INSIGHT
ST PET

Compact Guide: St Petersburg is the ultimate quick-reference guide to this fascinating destination. It tells you all you need to know about St Petersburg's attractions, from the grandeur of its imperial palaces to its elegant streets and squares, from its exquisite baroque churches to the overwhelming collections on show at the Hermitage.

This is one of more than 133 Compact Guides, which combine the interests and enthusiasms of two of the world's best known information providers: Insight Guides, whose titles have set the standard for visual travel guides since 1970, and Discovery Channel, the world's premier source of nonfiction television programming.

APA PUBLICATIONS
Part of the Langenscheidt Publishing Group

Insight Compact Guide: St Petersburg

Written by Dr Leonid Bloch
English version by Sarah Byrt
Updated by John Varoli
Photography by Anna Mockford and Nick Bonnetti
Additional photography by AKG London and Topham Picturepoint
Cover picture by Sylvain Grandadam/Robert Harding/Alamy
Edited by Siân Lezard
Design: Maria Lord
Picture Editor: Hilary Genin
Maps: Polyglott/Buchhaupt

Editorial Director: Brian Bell
Managing Editor: Tony Halliday

CONTACTING THE EDITORS: As every effort is made to provide accurate information in this publication, we would appreciate it if readers would call our attention to any errors and omissions by contacting:
Apa Publications, PO Box 7910, London SE1 1WE, England.
Fax: (44 20) 7403 0290
e-mail: insight@apaguide.co.uk

Information has been obtained from sources believed to be reliable, but its accuracy and completeness, and the opinions based thereon, are not guaranteed.

© 2004 APA Publications GmbH & Co. Verlag KG Singapore Branch, Singapore.

First Edition 1995. Second Edition 2002; Updated 2004
Printed in Singapore by Insight Print Services (Pte) Ltd
Original edition © Polyglott-Verlag Dr Bolte KG, Munich

Distributed in the UK & Ireland by:
GeoCenter International Ltd
The Viables Centre, Harrow Way, Basingstoke,
Hampshire RG22 4BJ
Tel: (44 1256) 817-987, fax: (44 1256) 817-988

Distributed in the United States by:
Langenscheidt Publishers, Inc.
46–35 54th Road, Maspeth, NY 11378
Tel: (1 718) 784-0055, fax: (1 718) 784-0640

Worldwide distribution enquiries:
APA Publications GmbH & Co. Verlag KG (Singapore Branch)
38 Joo Koon Road, Singapore 628990
Tel: (65) 6865-1600, Fax: (65) 6861-6438

www.insightguides.com

ST PETERSBURG

Introduction

Places

Culture

Travel Tips

◁ **Smolny Cathedral (p69)** Five onion domes tower above Rastrelli's baroque masterpiece.

▷ **The Hermitage (p87)** This world-famous museum contains a vast array of outstanding art.

▽ **Church on the Spilled Blood (p48)** A decorative riot of colour.

◁ **Catherine Palace (p103)** Rastrelli's lavish palace at Pushkin.

▽ **The Peter and Paul Fortress (p20)** The city's origin, founded in 1703.

△ **The Peterhof (p100)** Peter the Great built this magnificent palace, a Russian Versailles, 'befitting to the very highest of monarchs'; the Grand Cascade is stunning.

△ **Russian Museum (p50)** The world's largest collection of Russian art, ranging from medieval icons to modern art.

▽ **The Admiralty (p35)** One of the finest buildings in the city, the Admiralty reflects Russia's seafaring strength, documented by an abundance of sculptures and reliefs.

▽ **Winter Palace (p41)** Built for Tsarina Elisabeth between 1754 and 1762, this winter residence is a superb example of Russian baroque.

△ **The Mariinsky Theatre (p76)** This has played a pivotal role in Russian ballet and opera since it was built in 1860, and is the home of the Kirov Ballet Corps.

The Venice of the North

The second largest city in Russia and one of the world's major cities, St Petersburg has played a vital role in both Russian and European history. For two centuries it was the capital of the Russian Empire. Founded as St Petersburg (Russian: Sankt Peturburg) by Peter the Great in 1703, it was renamed Petrograd in 1914 and Leningrad in 1924. The name St Petersburg was restored in 1991.

St Petersburg was not only the stronghold of the tsars, but also of revolutionaries, and the city is renowned as the scene of the February and October revolutions of 1917. It is also renowned for the role it played in World War II, when for 872 days the local populace fiercely defended their city against the remorseless German siege.

In the decades following the war, St Petersburg was restored to its former glory. More recently, many of its buildings and monuments have been spruced up the city's 300th anniversary, which was celebrated in 2003.

Certainly, it is the architectural charm of St Petersburg, its elegance and harmony, which continues to make it so popular with visitors. The pleasingly symmetrical streets and squares, quiet canals and uniquely styled bridges provide a vivid contrast to the more untamed beauty of the surrounding countryside. Officially proclaimed the 'cultural capital of Russia', the city has a rich and varied cultural palette, offering much more than simply the Hermitage Museum and the Kirov Ballet of the Mariinsky Theatre. St Petersburg, along with Moscow, has more in the way of theatre, concerts, opera and pop than anywhere else in the country.

Opposite: St Isaac's Cathedral
Below: a unicorn on the Lomonosov Bridge
Bottom: the Red Bridge over the Moika Canal

RICH CULTURE

St Petersburg is also associated with many of the past greats of Russian culture. Among those who have lived and worked here on their immortal creations are poets and writers such as Pushkin, Dostoyevsky and Gogol, the Realist painter

👁 **White Nights**

In summer, the White Nights (during which the sun barely sets) are most apparent from the beginning of June to early July. During this time the city has a very particular magic. The steeples of the cathedrals, the tips of the city towers, and windows of the palaces and churches shine in what seems to be an unending twilight; even at night, downtown St Petersburg is full of people.

From November until the end of March the Neva and its canals are mostly frozen.

The city is one of the great centres of classical ballet

Repin, the composers Tchaikovsky and Glinka, as well as the architect Rastrelli. Stage artists such as Kommissarzhevskaya, Chaliapin and Pavlova have performed in the city's theatres.

In St Petersburg, where the first Russian Academy of Sciences was founded on the orders of Peter the Great, there are now over 300,000 students, studying at 47 universities and 92 technical colleges. There are more than 200 museums, 2,600 libraries and 300 scientific research institutes.

It would be naive to assume that it is possible to obtain a complete picture of Russia by means of one or even several trips. Consequently, it is necessary to select from the rich geography of this country. However, no visit to Russia which excludes a tour of St Petersburg can hope to provide an adequate picture of the history and culture of this country, of its customs and traditions, its greatness and its beauty.

LOCATION AND SIZE

The city is located on the delta of the Neva River at the head of the Gulf of Finland, at 60°N and 30°E, on the same latitude as southern Alaska, the southernmost point of Greenland, and Oslo. St Petersburg spreads across some 44 islands of the delta and across neighbouring parts of the floodplain. The city has always been prone to flooding because of its flat and low-lying terrain, but this has been alleviated by the construction of a dyke across the Gulf of Finland. No fewer than 60 rivers, streams and canals, with a total length of over 160km (100 miles), pass through the city and surrounding area. These make St Petersburg a city of waterways and bridges and have earned it the nickname 'Venice of the North'.

Flowing out of Lake Ladoga to the east, the Neva itself is only 74km (46 miles) long. Within St Petersburg, this river and its various tributaries divide the central part of the city into four distinct sections. The Admiralty Side, where much of the city's historical and cultural heritage is concentrated, runs along the left (south) bank of the Neva. Between the two major arms of the Neva, the Bolshaya (Great) and Malaya (Little) Neva, is Vasilievsky Island. The Malaya Neva and its tributary known as the Bolshaya Nevka enclose a group of islands known as the Petrograd Side; the Vyborg Side constitutes part of the mainland to the east.

The city covers an area of 606 sq km (234 sq miles), although Greater St Petersburg, forming a horseshoe shape around the Gulf of Finland and encompassing such historic towns as Oranienbaum and Peterhof in the west, as well as Kurortny District on the north shore, is much larger.

CLIMATE

St Petersburg has a moderate, maritime climate, which is the mildest to be found on this latitude in Russia. The warmest month is July (average temperature: 18°C/64°F), the coldest January (average temperature: –8°C/18°F). Generally, there is snow from the beginning of November to the middle of April, though there are winters without much snow.

The weather in St Petersburg is never particularly stable: the temperature can fluctuate up to 6°C (43°F) between the different areas of the town. The Gulf of Finland's bathing season lasts

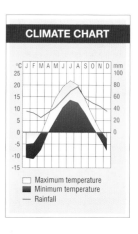

CLIMATE CHART

☐ Maximum temperature
■ Minimum temperature
— Rainfall

Sunset over the Gulf of Finland

from the middle of June until the end of August; the water temperature during this time ranges from 14–24°C (57–75°F).

The White Nights are in June, so called for obvious reasons – the sun barely sets below the horizon *(see panel on page 8)*.

THE DREAM OF PETER THE GREAT

Below: Peter the Great
Bottom: looking along the canal to the Church on the Spilled Blood

St Petersburg is recognised as one of the most beautiful cities in the world. However, it should not be forgotten that its magnificent buildings are also the visible expression of absolute power. Peter the Great used brute force to realise his dream of creating a city from the unhealthy Neva marshland. A demonstration of power and the repercussions of the tsar's traumatic childhood were decisive factors contributing towards the founding of St Petersburg. As a child, Peter the Great had been eyewitness to gruesome massacres in the Kremlin; these left him with both a horror of Moscow and a nervous disorder.

Of course, there was also a political motive for the founding of St Petersburg: the access that the city would provide to the Baltic, the window to the West. To achieve this goal, Peter allied himself with the Danes and Poles against the Swedes, who occupied the area around the Neva estuary.

At the beginning of the Great Northern War

(1700–21) the Russians seized hold of the Swedish Fortress Noteborg, one of Novgorod's outposts during the Middle Ages. They renamed it Schlüsselburg and subsequently settled down in the nearby Neva Delta. The first defence was a very simple construction. On 16 May 1703 Peter the Great personally laid the foundation stone for the Peter and Paul Fortress on Hare Island (Zayachi Ostrov); this was followed in 1704 by the foundation stone for the Admiralty. In order to defend these buildings against attack from the sea, Kronstadt fortress was built on Kotlin Island. When his troops subsequently conquered King Charles XII of Sweden's hitherto invincible army, Peter the Great saw the victory as confirmation of his strategy.

ARCHITECTURAL WHOLE

The tsar was the first European potentate to conceive and organise his city as an architectural whole. Having first dreamt of having the city modelled on Amsterdam, Peter the Great changed his mind during a trip to France, and chose the French architect Leblond to draft ground plans for the new city.

Creating one of the world's most beautiful cities from the barren swamp required hundreds of thousands of workers. Swedish prisoners-of-war, Finns and Russian serfs were brought in as forced labourers; they drove stakes into the marshy ground and transported blocks of granite and stone to the site with their bare hands.

Due to the shortage of masons, it was, for many years, forbidden to build in stone in any city other than St Petersburg. Every barge and ship importing goods to the city had to carry a certain amount of stone aboard, and every citizen owning more than 500 serfs was obliged to build a two-storey stone building in St Petersburg at his own expense. The town was often destroyed by flooding, but each time it was rebuilt, bigger and better than before.

In order to populate the tsar's new city, a *ukaz* (decree) was issued, as of 1712, commanding people from all over the Russian empire to move to St Petersburg.

> **Absolute monarch**
> Peter the Great loved to make decisions for his subjects, even in their private affairs. In the same way that he would make political decisions, he would also make decisions about the wearing of beards, the height of chimneys, the arrangement of parties, etc. On the one hand this resulted in stamping an absolutist seal on his reign, yet on the other it brought his country out of the Middle Ages and into the modern era with a western European flair.

The Raphael Loggia in the Hermitage

CENTRE OF LEARNING

The tsar did not only want to leave a shining example of architectural creation to posterity; his autocratic standards were such that he wanted to breathe intellectual life into his work too. St Petersburg was to become a centre of learning. With the help of Leibnitz, the German rationalist philosopher and mathematician, he worked on a project for the creation of an Academy of Sciences and various institutes. It was planned that foreign professors would educate Russian students here, and at the same time young Russians would be sent abroad to study at universities in western Europe.

Chesma Church red; Mariinsky green; Smolny Cathedral blue; Menchikov Palace yellow

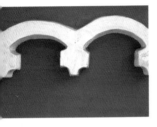

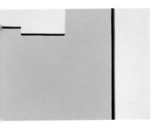

St Petersburg was soon ranked alongside Paris and Rome as one of the most beautiful cities in the world. It was regarded, with some justification, as the complete work of an absolute ruler whose superhuman efforts had brought the Russian empire to the forefront of the international scene.

The reign of Elisabeth Petrovna, daughter of Peter the Great, saw the construction of the Winter Palace by Italian architect Bartolomo Rastrelli, the Smolny Cathedral and the enormous Catherine Palace in Tsarskoe Selo, which until its almost total destruction during World War II, ranked as one of the most magnificent baroque buildings in Europe.

CATHERINE AND HER SUCCESSORS

The grandeur of the city was augmented again by Catherine II, the wife of Peter III (nephew and heir to Elisabeth, who was deposed and murdered in 1762). During her reign the transition from baroque to Classicism began: Rinaldi created the Marble Palace, the Pavlovsk Palace was begun by Cameron, the Academy of Fine Arts was built by Vallin de la Mothe. Catherine was held by the intellectual elite of Europe to be a well-educated and committed ruler, an enlightened autocrat who conducted lengthy correspondences with Voltaire and other philosophers. At the same time, she had all those who tried to realise the ideas of these philosophers thrown into the dungeons of the Peter and Paul Fortress. Using architects, sculptors and well-diggers brought from France and Italy, the empress completely remodelled the Neva Islands; she had wide avenues and spacious parks laid out, large and small palaces built. The Winter Palace was completed, the Small Hermitage was built, and construction of the second (Old) Hermitage was started.

Paul I, her successor, lacked the capacity of his extraordinary mother both domestically and in foreign policy. His only major architectural contribution was the Mikhailovsky, or Engineering Castle, which he had built to protect him from conspirators. He could have saved himself the expense though, since he was murdered there 40 days after moving in.

Alexander I's role as head of the coalition formed against Napoleon made St Petersburg the diplomatic capital of Europe. During his reign the Italian architect Carlo Rossi built many elaborate yellow and white palaces, including: the General Staff Building, the two pavilions of the Anichkov Palace, as well as the marvellous Arts Square, bordered by the Mikhail Palace and other impressive Rossi creations.

Although subsequent tsars commissioned new buildings in St Petersburg, these were no longer

Revolutions

In the 18th century, St Petersburg was plagued by palace intrigue and coups. Most notably, Catherine the Great came to power by deposing her husband, Peter III. But Paul's death was the last successful palace coup, and in the 19th century the tsars were more concerned with suppressing organized popular revolution.

The facade of the General Staff building

Siege mentality
The people of St Petersburg take great pride in their city, even in the face of overwhelming adversity. Not surprisingly, they did not abandon the city during World War II's Siege of Leningrad, as it was then called, but fought on when the city was not only encircled by the Nazis, but practically forgotten by Russia's communist leaders in Moscow who, some historians claim, sought to punish the city's inhabitants for their opposition to Stalin.

as unified and accomplished as in the earlier years. The days of the well-balanced architectural ensemble were over. The tsars had other worries: the Decembrists' revolt was the first sign of the empire's vulnerability and Palace Square was now the arena for portentous events *(see pages 16–7).*

POLITICS AND ECONOMY

Together with the Ukraine and Belorussia, Russia represents the historic core of the once-great Russian Empire which ended with the October Revolution in 1917. Even after the disintegration of the Soviet Union in 1991, the country remains by far the largest of the former Soviet Socialist Republics.

As a result of the democratisation that followed Mikhail Gorbachev's *Perestroika* (restructuring), begun in 1986, as well as the failed coup of communist hardliners in August 1991, an almost 75-year-old Communist dictatorship came to an end as did its corresponding Soviet state system. Since then there have been enormous changes. A one-party state has been transformed into a fledgling democracy, and a socialist-planned economy – and all the stability that went with it – has had to give way to the forces of the free market.

A revolutionary painting from the Artillery Museum

The workings of the free market have had a huge effect on all Russians. The immediate effects of the freeing of prices in 1992 were a plummeting rouble and rampant inflation. Despite the 1998 crash, the Russian economy is recovering (thanks in large part to high oil prices), and in 2003 posted its highest growth since the end of communism.

Many co-operative and small private companies have been established, shops and restaurants have proliferated and, within the framework of joint-venture agreements, Russian and foreign firms have merged to work with one another. There is now an emerging moneyed middle class, with increasing numbers of people able to buy an apartment, a car and travel abroad.

LOCAL INDUSTRY

St Petersburg has long enjoyed international acclaim for its industries, which include shipbuilding, electrical engineering, chemicals, textiles, leather, fur and food, and the production of electronic, optical and other precision apparatus. The St Petersburg seaport is the country's second largest and, even though the Gulf of Finland freezes over during the winter, icebreakers keep the port open all year round.

PEOPLE

St Petersburg is the most northerly city in the world to have more than 1 million inhabitants. Today, more than 5 million people live here, not only Russians, who make up the vast majority of the population, but also Ukrainians, Belorussians and representatives from many other nations of Russia and the former Soviet Republics. The atmosphere of old St Petersburg may be long gone, but in this city designed as a cultural centre, many of the citizens consider themselves to be the most cultivated of Russians. In keeping with the city's traditional role as Russia's window to the world, the inhabitants maintain a cosmopolitan outlook, ready to deal with the vast changes coming their way.

Below: a giant crane at the sea terminal
Bottom: workers at the Aleksandrinsky Theatre

HISTORICAL HIGHLIGHTS

Pre-10th century The region around the future city is inhabited by Slav tribes.

10th century The Slavs join with the Kievan Russians. Their main trade route runs through the Gulf of Finland, along the Neva and across Lake Ladoga.

12th century The region becomes part of the Novgorod feudal republic. Its good geographical position attracts attention from neighbours in the north.

13th–14th century The Swedish kings try on many occasions to annex the area.

1617 Sweden occupies the banks of the Neva and sets up the Nyenschanz Fortress. Russia is cut off from the Baltic.

1700 The beginning of the Great Northern War between Russia and Sweden. Russia tries to regain access to the Baltic.

1702 The Swedish Noteborg Fortress is recaptured. This is key to the founding of the future city of St Petersburg.

1703 The Nyenschanz Fortress falls to the Russians. Peter I commissions the Saint Peter Fortress on Zayachi Ostrov. St Petersburg is founded at the same time. Factories and various industries are established. The first newspapers and magazines appear, the maritime academy opens (1715), followed by artillery, engineering and medical schools, the first museum (1719) and the science academy (1725).

1721 Russia wins the Great Northern War. Peter I (the Great) becomes the country's leading spiritual and secular power.

1724 Tsar Peter I moves the state institutions to the new city. St Petersburg becomes the official capital of Russia and most court-related families move there.

1725 Peter I dies and his heirs, Catherine I, Peter II and Anna Ivanovna, ignore the state, but spare no expense on luxuries. His daughter Elisabeth (1741–61) and Catherine II (the Great) – born Princess von Anhalt-Zerbst (1763–96) – continue with his plan. They summon the best Russian and foreign architects to St Petersburg.

19th century The secret Northern Company forms at the beginning of the century aiming to end the autocracy of the tsar and abolish serfdom. The exceptional luxury in which the aristocracy lives is in stark contrast to the unbelievable poverty of the working population.

1812 The Russians defeat Napoleon's Grande Armée and large memorials are erected in St Petersburg.

1824 The biggest flood in the history of the city does tremendous damage.

1825 The 'Decembrist Uprising'. Aristocratic officers and 3,000 soldiers and sailors try to force the tsar Nikolai (Nicholas) I to abdicate his rights to the throne, but are ruthlessly suppressed.

1837 The first Russian railway, links St Petersburg with Tsarskoe Selo.

1851 Regular train services begin between St Petersburg and Moscow.

1861 Official abolition of serfdom. Public opinion is roused by leaflets, magazines and by the work of revolutionary artists. There are an increasing number of assassinations. The prisons are full and there are numerous deportations.

1879 In St Petersburg the revolutionary Narodnaya Volya (People's Will) is founded, which organises the assassination of Tsar Alexander II on 1 March 1881.

1890 Lenin's first trip to St Petersburg where he completes his legal studies.

1893 A single, large movement forms under the leadership of Lenin and his party. They begin the political education of the workers in the factories, built both south of the Narva Triumphal Arch and in the northern quarter of the city.

1895 Lenin sets up the Union for the Struggle for the Liberation of the Working Class in St Petersburg. From this, the proletarian revolutionary party emerges.

1905 A strike breaks out in the Putilov Works, supported by other industries in the city. 140,000 workers march to the Winter Palace with a petition. Troops kill more than 100 marchers and wound hundreds more. This sparks a general revolt, joined by some sections of the army and navy. The tsar is obliged to make a few concessions, withdrawn soon afterwards, including the establishment of the Duma (State Assembly) with very limited rights.

1914 The German-sounding St Petersburg is changed to the Russian Petrograd.

1917 World War I brings Russia to the brink of economic and political collapse. During the February Revolution, Nicholas II abdicates. In Petrograd the Provisional Government, led by Kerensky, calls for the continuation of war against Germany. Lenin arrives in Petrograd from exile in Switzerland to turn this middle-class revolt into a proletarian revolution. However, after his defeat in July, he is pursued by the Provisional Government, and goes into hiding. On 10 October the Bolshevik Central Committee decide on an armed revolt. On 25 October they gain control of the insurgent Petrograd.

1918 In March the Brest-Litovsk peace treaty is signed and the government moves back to Moscow. On Lenin's death

(1924) Petrograd becomes Leningrad.

1941–4 German troops encircle Leningrad. On 8 September rail links are cut and the *Blokada* (siege) – which lasts for 872 days – begins. Several hundred thousand people are evacuated from Leningrad via the 'Road of Life' – the only route connecting the city with the mainland. During the winter of 1941–2 temperatures reach –35°C (–31°F), and 650,000 people starve and freeze to death. The siege is lifted on January 27 and the people of St Petersburg set about rebuilding their city.

1950 The city's production levels reach pre-war levels. The Kirov Stadium is built.

1955 The first metro station is opened.

1965 20 years after the war, Leningrad is honoured as the 'City of Valour'.

1986 Mikhail Gorbachev begins the policies of *Perestroika* (restructuring) and *Glasnost* (openness).

1991 Boris Yeltsin president of Russia. In August a coup is suppressed in Leningrad. After a referendum the city is renamed St Petersburg. Gorbachev resigns and the USSR ceases to exist.

1996 Yeltsin narrowly defeats Gennady Zyuganov in the presidential elections.

1998 Nicholas II and his family are buried in the Cathedral of St Petersburg's Peter and Paul Fortress. The rouble crashes leading to galloping inflation.

2000 Vladimir Putin, having become prime minister in 1999, is elected president of the federation.

2003 The city celebrates its 300th anniversary.

2004 Vladimir Putin is re-elected.

1: Peter and Paul Fortress and Beyond

Peter and Paul Fortress – Petrograd Side – Vasilievsky Island

Maps below & page 25

Previous page: reflections in Palace Square
Below: the cathedral spire seen over the fortress wall

The Petrograd Side (Petrogradskaya Storona) of St Petersburg encompasses the islands of Hare, Petrograd, Apothecary and Peter. It was on Zayachy Ostrov (Hare Island) that Peter the Great is said to have laid the foundation stone for the ★★★ **Peter and Paul Fortress** ❶ (Petropavlovskaya Krepost, open Thur–Tues 11am–5pm; closed Wed; grounds open every night until 10pm).

From the city centre, now located on the left bank of the Neva, take the underground to Gorkovskaya station. Or you can walk across the Troitsky Bridge, from where there are beautiful views across the river to the Palace Embankment and to Vasilievsky Island in the west.

HISTORY

Built to protect Russia, the fortress did not actually see active combat until 25 October 1917. For more than 200 years the cannons did not fire a single shot. However, not even 10 years had gone by before the fortress had been transformed into a dreaded prison. One of the first political prisoners was Peter I's son; Tsarevich Aleksei was suspected of participating in a conspiracy against his father. He died under torture in 1718.

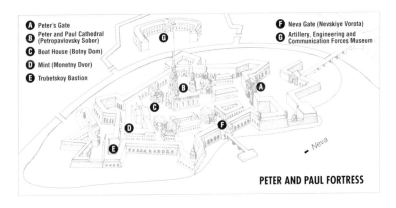

Ⓐ Peter's Gate
Ⓑ Peter and Paul Cathedral (Petropavlovsky Sobor)
Ⓒ Boat House (Botny Dom)
Ⓓ Mint (Monetny Dvor)
Ⓔ Trubetskoy Bastion
Ⓕ Neva Gate (Nevskiye Vorota)
Ⓖ Artillery, Engineering and Communication Forces Museum

Neva

PETER AND PAUL FORTRESS

The first Russian aristocratic political dissident, the writer Alexander Radischev, author of *A Journey from St Petersburg to Moscow*, awaited his execution here in 1790. The death sentence was lifted at the last moment and Catherine II gave orders that the prisoner was to serve 10 years in Siberian exile.

The leaders of the Decembrists' Revolt, Bestushev-Rumin, Pestel and Rileyev, were imprisoned in the Secret House of the Alekseyev trench, the prison for hardened criminals. The novelist Dostoyevsky, the revolutionary democrat, philosopher, critic and writer Chernyshevky and the writer Pisarev also served sentences here. The vast majority of the convicted revolutionaries of the 1880s sat in the cells of the Trubetskoy Bastion, among others the members of the Narodnaya Volya Party.

It was in the casemate of this fortress that the last meeting between Lenin's mother and his elder brother took place. Lenin's brother, Alexander, was executed 10 days later for his participation in the assassination attempt on Tsar Alexander III. In January 1905 Gorky, a proletarian writer close to Lenin and the Bolsheviks, was brought to this prison. Suffering from tuberculosis, it was here that he wrote his play *Child of the Sun*. The Trubetskoy Bastion has been preserved exactly as it was in 1872. In 1922 the fortress became a museum.

FORTRESS TOUR

Turn left after the Troitsky Bridge and cross another small bridge (Ioann Bridge or Ioannovsky Most) to reach St John's Gate (Ioannovskye Vorota) and then **St Peter's Gate Ⓐ** (Petrovskye Vorota), leading into the fortress. This triumphal arch was built according to plans by Trezzini in 1718, and is the only such structure from the period to survive. Statues of Bellona (god of war) and Minerva (goddess of wisdom, the arts and crafts) were placed in the niches of the gate to symbolise the wisdom of Peter I.

Star Attraction
● Peter and Paul Fortress

Missing persons
Some of the Romanovs themselves, not the tsar's immediate family but a number of Great Princes who were uncles and cousins, ended up imprisoned in the Peter and Paul Fortress after the 1917 Revolution. They were executed early in 1918, and their bodies thrown into a ditch somewhere on the fortress territory, unknown to this day.

Bathing alongside the fortress

Maps
on pages
20 & 25

Burial rites

The Peter and Paul Fortress held its most recent tsarist burial in July 1998 when the remains of Nicholas II, the Empress Alexandra, three of their daughters, and two servants were buried in the Peter and Paul Cathedral. The remains of the tsarevich, Alexei, and daughter, Anastasia, have never been found, and stories persist about their supposed escape from execution at the hands of the Bolsheviks.

Peter and Paul Cathedral spire

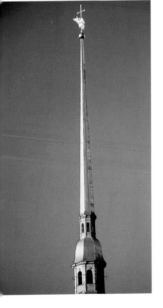

PETER AND PAUL CATHEDRAL

From Peter's Gate a straight alley leads to what is, from an art historian's point of view, the most valuable monument in the fortress, the ★★★ **Peter and Paul Cathedral** (Petropavlovsky Sobor) **B**, which was built between 1712–32, also according to the plans of Trezzini. The centrepiece of the fortress, the cathedral is considered to be a good example of 18th-century Russian architecture, modelled on the Dutch and German styles. The interior is 61m (200ft) long and 16m (52ft) high; the bell tower is 122m (400ft) high. The carved, gold iconostasis (the screen decorated with icons separating the sanctuary from the nave) is regarded as one of the most superb examples of Russian wood-carving in existence. Taking five years to complete, the iconostasis was modelled from sketches drawn up by Zarudny.

The cathedral contains the white-marble tombs of the Russian tsars with the exception of Peter II and Ivan VI. In July 1998 the burial took place for the bodies of the executed Nicholas II and his family. Even today, fresh flowers are regularly placed on the tomb of Peter I. The imperial eagle, in gilded bronze, decorates only the Romanov tombs, the rulers of Russia for 300 years. To the right of the southern entrance it is hard to miss the two enormous tombs made of Altai jasper and Urals rhodonite. They are those of Tsar Alexander II and his wife, the Hessian princess Maria Alexandrovna. Every 15 minutes the old Dutch clock (restored in 1987) chimes from the belltower built between 1762 and 1766.

BOAT HOUSE AND MINT

Next to the cathedral stands a beautiful columned pavilion, crowned by a sculpture of the sea goddess. This is the **Boat House** **C** (Botny Dom), which once housed the small English boat that Peter the Great learned to sail in on the River Jausa. Peter I's boat is described as the 'Grandfather of the Russian fleet'. Today it can be seen in the Central Naval Museum on Vasilievsky Island (*see page 27*).

In the west wing of the fortress is the **Mint**
(Monetny Dvor), installed in the fortress on Peter
I's command in 1724. The present buildings were
built between 1798 and 1806 by Antonio Porto.
In the days of the tsar, gold, silver and copper
coins were minted here; today, coins and medals
are made, as were the pennants carried by Russian spaceships to the moon, Mars and Venus.

Behind the Mint is the **Trubetskoy Bastion** **E**
(see page 21).

NEVA GATE

Leading out to the Captain's harbour the **Neva
Gate** **F** (Nevskaya Vorota), in the south of the
fortress, has a very colourful past. It was also
called Death Gate, because prisoners sentenced
to death were – if not executed there and then –
led through this gate to the boat which was to take
them to their place of execution. Every day at
noon a cannon is fired here.

The cannon were not always used for such
peaceful purposes. In October 1917 the garrison
soldiers joined with the insurgents. On 25 October, the headquarters ordered that the Winter
Palace be stormed after a cannon shot was fired
from the *Aurora* cruiser during the night. It was
under the covering fire of the Peter and Paul
Fortress that the Provisional Government was

Star Attraction
● **Peter and Paul Cathedral**

*Below: the cathedral nave
Bottom: view from the fortress
over the Neva to the city*

Maps on pages 20 & 25

Below: from the Museum of Political History
Bottom: Peter's coat of arms, by Peter the Great's Cabin

toppled. For the first time in 214 years, the fortress took part in active combat.

There are two other permanent exhibitions within the grounds of the Peter and Paul Fortress: **Petrograd's History from 1703–1917** and **The Architecture of St Petersburg-Petrograd**; both are part of the Museum of the History of St Petersburg (open 11am–5pm; closed Wed).

PLACE OF EXECUTION

To the left of the Ioann Bridge, when leaving the Peter and Paul Fortress, an obelisk is visible on the other side of the canal. It was here that the ill-fated Decembrists were executed (*see page 17*). During the hanging the rope broke three times, with the result that one of the three prisoners concerned broke a leg. However, as opposed to revoking the death penalty, as was customary under such circumstances, the men were hanged a second time.

Within the grounds of the fortress is the Gothic-styled red building of the former arsenal, which now houses the ★ **Artillery Museum** G (open Wed–Sun 11am–5pm; closed last Thur of the month). Founded by Peter the Great in 1703, the weapon collection currently contains approximately 70,000 exhibits. It ranges from 15th-century swords to 20th-century ballistic missiles, and includes Lenin's armoured car.

PETROGRAD SIDE

To the east of the Peter and Paul Fortress, on the Petrograd side, is **Troitskaya Ploshchad** ❷. On the left side of the square (Kronverksky Prospekt 1/2) is the villa of the former prima ballerina, Mathilde Kshessinskaya, who was famous not only for her dancing but also for her affair with the tsarevich, who became Tsar Nicholas II. In March 1917 **Kshessinskaya Mansion** was used as the Bolshevik Party headquarters, and Lenin addressed the crowds from the balcony. Built by Gogen in 1904–6, and a good example of the Style Moderne, it now houses the ★ **Museum of Russian**

Political History ❸ (formerly the October Revolution Museum), where various changing exhibitions are held. There is also a permanent display about the ballerina herself, as well as a new wax exhibition on the gruesome death of Tsar Nicholas II and his family (open 10am–6pm; closed Thur).

PETER THE GREAT'S CABIN

To the southeast of Troitskaya Ploshchad (Petrovskaya Naberezhnaya 6) is the **Cabin of Peter the Great ❹** (Muzey-domik Petra I; open Wed–Mon 10am–5pm; closed Tues and last Mon of the month). This was the city's first domestic residence; it was built by soldiers in a few days in May 1703. From here Peter the Great could observe the construction of the fortress and other buildings. The captain and crew of the first foreign ship to bring wares to St Petersburg were given 5,000 gold roubles by the tsar (who piloted the sloop that came out to meet them). This Dutch ship was renamed *Petersburg* and sailed the same route for another 50 years.

> **Modesty personified**
> Peter the Great, though tsar over a powerful empire, shunned the luxury usually preferred by royalty. He was known for his simple tastes, lack of formality, and for helping out with the menial labour to build his city and the Russian navy. The small size of Peter's houses shocked foreign visitors, and even Peter's deputy, Menshikov, built himself a grander palace.

THE *AURORA*

Following the road east along the river, the road bends towards the quay, where the famous

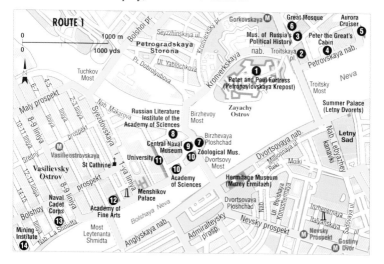

Map on page 25

Below: sailors on board the Aurora
Bottom: the Aurora *at anchor*

★*Aurora* **cruiser** ❺ (Kreyser Avrora) is anchored. Launched in 1903, the ship is now a branch of the Central Naval Museum (open 10.30am–4pm; closed Mon and Fri).

The cruiser, built in St Petersburg in 1897–1900, took an active part in the Russo-Japanese War of 1904–5. It participated in the battle at Tsushima Bay, during which most of Russia's Pacific fleet was destroyed. In February 1917 the crew of the cruiser hoisted the ship's red flag for the first time. From then on the *Aurora* was an important mobile support of the Bolsheviks in their fight against the Kerensky government.

During the night of 25 October, the cruiser sailed into the Neva and trained its guns on the Winter Palace, residence of the Provisional Government. At 9.45pm the forward gun of the *Aurora* fired a blank shot, giving the signal for the Winter Palace to be stormed. The victorious leader of the putsch, Lenin, immediately transmitted a declaration to the citizens of the revolution over the ship radio, informing them of the proceedings. After World War I the *Aurora* became a training ship. During World War II the guns were used once again, this time against the German enemy laying siege to the town.

On the other side of the Great Neva on the Pirogovskaya Embankment is a modern building housing the St Petersburg Hotel.

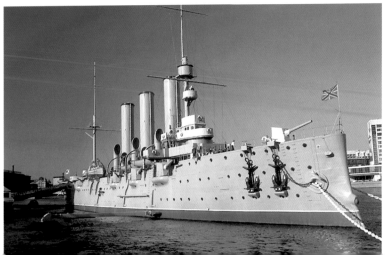

GREAT MOSQUE

Back in Troitskaya Ploshchad in the north one can see the two slim minarets and blue-tiled dome of the **Great Mosque** ❻ (Mechet), the only mosque in St Petersburg. It was built in 1912 by S. Kritschinskiy and Vasilyev using funds provided by the Islamic community and was modelled on the Gur-Emir Shrine in Samarkand. There were many Muslim Tatars and Kalmucks living in the town even during Peter the Great's reign. They were regarded as being among his most trusted servants.

The interior of the building is decorated in accordance with Islamic tradition: the columns are layered in green marble, and Koranic verses are engraved on the enormous chandeliers in the middle of the room. After extensive renovation, the Mosque is once again open for prayers.

The Kronverksky Prospekt curves round the Aleksandrovsky Sad (Alexander Park) in a wide semicircle, inside which is the ★ **Zoo** and the planetarium. The Prospekt ends near Birzhevoi Most (Stock-Exchange Bridge), which links the Petrograd side with Vasilievsky Island. Turning off right shortly before the bridge is Prospekt Dobrolyubova and the modern buildings of the Yubileyny sports complex.

VASILIEVSKY ISLAND

Located on the tip of Vasilievsky Island are what are considered to be the finest examples of architecture in St Petersburg. This island, opposite the Admiralty and the Angliskaya (English) Embankment, and encircled by the Great and Little Neva as well as the Smolyenka River, is the largest island in the Neva Delta. The spit, known as the Strelka, juts out into the river in the east where the Great Neva divides with the Little Neva, and from here there is a magnificent view.

EXCHANGE SQUARE

The Strelka is taken up by ★★ **Birzhevaya Ploshchad** ❼ (Stock Exchange Square). On the

Star Attraction
● Stock Exchange Square

👁 **Trusted workers**
Muslims were among the most trusted workers in tsarist times because they were considered reliable, disciplined, hardworking, and most important they did not drink. Russian workers, then as now, had a big weakness for consuming large amounts of vodka and other spirits, which is the main culprit in declining life expectancies even today.

The Great Mosque

Map on page 25

Below: one of the Rostral Columns
Bottom: facade of the Naval Museum

slope down to the Neva on both sides of the large semi-circular square in front of the Stock Exchange are the two Doric-styled **Rostral Columns** (Rostralni Kolony; 1810, by Thomas de Thomon). These 32-m (105-ft) columns were originally built as signal towers, and navigational flares were burnt on the capitals. They lit the way for the ships to the Neva moorings. Later the fires were replaced by gas lights, still lit today on national holidays. In accordance with ancient Roman tradition, the columns were decorated with ships' prows, which for the sake of the symbolism were sawn off from captured enemy vessels. At the foot of the columns colossal figures represent Russia's great trade rivers – the Volga, Dnieper, Volkhov and Neva.

LITERATURE INSTITUTE

The Strelka used to be the main city harbour. After the main harbour was moved to the west bank of Vasilievsky Island at the beginning of the 19th century, the old harbour buildings were put to other uses. The former Customs House (by Luchini and Stasov, 1832), built in the style of late Russian Classicism, now houses the **Russian Literature Institute of the Academy of Sciences** ❽ (Institut Russkoi Literatury, open Mon–Fri 10am–6pm; closed Sat and Sun). The palatial

rooms of the Institute (4 Naberezhnaya Makarova), commonly called Pushkin House (Pushkinsky Dom), contain a variety of interesting archival material such as letters and samples of handwriting of almost all the most significant Russian authors of the 18th and 19th century.

The exhibition at the museum shows the development of Russian literature from the first edition of the ancient Russian epic *The Song of Igor's Campaign* up to the present day.

CENTRAL NAVAL MUSEUM

The **Naval Museum** ❾ (Voenno Morskoy Muzey, open Wed–Sun 11am–6pm; closed Mon, Tues and last Thur of the month), is housed in the former stock exchange (1804–11, by Thomas de Thomon). The building is a copy of the Greek temple of Paestum. It is surrounded by a peristyle with 44 Doric columns; the enormous staircase leads to the main floor of the former stock exchange. Since 1940 it has contained the Central Naval Museum.

The foundation for the collection was provided by Peter the Great, who started collecting ship models in 1709. Among the 800,000 exhibits are 1,500 models of ships that served in the Russian fleet. As mentioned earlier, the museum also contains Peter I's boat *(see page 22)*.

ZOOLOGICAL MUSEUM

West of the Strelka, stretching along the south of Vasilievsky Island between the Palace Bridge and the Nikolayevsky Bridge, is the University Embankment (Universitetskaya Naberezhnaya). The warehouses at No 1 have been turned into the **Zoological Museum** ❿ (Zoologichesky Muzey; open 11am–5pm; closed Fri). The museum has one of the world's largest natural history collections, containing over 10 million specimens of insects, 185,000 specimens of fish, and 88,000 mammals. There are also numerous mammoth carcasses, but the highlight is the stuffed mammoth, which lived over 44,000 years ago, found in the permafrost of Yakntsia, Siberia, in 1901.

Small beginnings
The Russian navy is among the youngest in Europe, and rarely distinguished itself in battle in tsarist times. In fact, a large portion of it was easily obliterated by Japan in 1904–5. But during the 1960s the leaders of the Soviet Union spent enormous amounts to build an offensive, blue-water fleet second only to that of the United States.

A Soviet star on the Naval Museum

Map
on page
25

Below: the university
Bottom: the Kunstkamera

Worth particular attention is the former Kunst-kamera, which was founded by Peter I and now contains the **Museum of Anthropology and Ethnography** (Muzei Antropologii i Etnografii), and a museum dedicated to Lomonosov, the learned chemist, physicist, geologist and gram-marian (1711–65). Before Lomonosov worked in these rooms, they were used to house the exhibits of the first natural science museum, commis-sioned by Peter I.

Visitors came to admire the astronomical instru-ments, maps, rare books, minerals and other things collected in part by the tsars themselves. In order to encourage visits from citizens who did not yet know what a museum was, there was no charge and foreign visitors received a glass of vodka at the entrance. Among the exhibits in the **Lomonosov Museum** (Muzei Lomonosova) is the so-called Gottorp Globe, which is over 3m (10ft) wide.

ACADEMY OF SCIENCES

When at the end of the 18th century the former academy building had been outgrown by its exhibits, a new academy building, the **Academy of Sciences** (Akademiya Nauka), designed by Quarenghi, was built in Classical style next door (1788). It is very different from the Kunstkamera and the adjoining buildings which are in the char-

acteristic baroque style of the early 18th century. Stretching along the Neva, the main facade of this three-storey building is adorned with a monumental portal consisting of eight Ionic columns.

Inside, the palatial staircase and white conference room, with its 18th- and 19th-century furnishings, are both well worth seeing. Next to the academy building is a bronze memorial to Lomonosov (by Sveschikov and Petrov).

The former seat of the 12 ministries of state *(kollegy)* is now **St Petersburg University ⓫** (St Petersburgsky Gosudarstvenny Universitet). Around 20,000 students are currently studying at its 15 colleges. Designed by Trezzini, the building was constructed between 1722–41 as a complex with 12 identically large buildings.

Not originally intended as a university, the building was the seat of the 12 *kollegi*, (ministries furnished according to the needs of Peter the Great). In 1830 the buildings were affiliated to the university, founded by Alexander I a few years earlier (1819). Inside, only Peter's Room has been preserved in its original form, though it is not open to the public.

> **Alexander Menshikov**
> Alexander Menshikov was born into a non-noble family in Moscow, but became the close friend and confidant of Peter the Great, who was impressed with his ability. Menshikov served Russia as Field Marshall and senior statesman, and basically ruled Russia from 1725-27, after Peter's death and during the reign of Catherine I, Peter's wife. Menshikov tried to marry his daughter to Peter II, Peter the Great's son, but the former was quickly deposed and Menshikov finished his life in exile in Siberia.

MENSHIKOV PALACE

On the embankment are three other buildings dating from the 18th century which have belonged to the university at various points. The first house (No 11) is Tsar Peter II's former palace; the second (No 13) was used as headquarters for the first officer cadets; and the yellow building (No 15), which has the date 1710 inscribed on the gable, is the **★ Menshikov Palace**, an ornately styled baroque building. The tsar was accustomed to entertaining foreign ambassadors in lavish style here.

This palace was one of St Petersburg's first stone houses and is now part of the Hermitage Museum *(see page 87)*. Having made a gift of the house and the entire island to his closest advisor Menshikov in 1701, Peter the Great then took it back in 1714. Today its exhibits reflect Russian culture during the reign of Peter I (open Tues–Sun 10.30am–5.30pm; closed Mon).

The Menshikov Palace

Map on page 25

Egyptian connection
In front of the main facade of the Academy of Fine Arts is a quay, constructed in strict Classical style (1834, by Thon). The granite statues of the sphinxes originally came from Thebes, the capital of ancient Egypt. For this reason the mooring is also called the Sphinx Quay.

FINE ARTS ACADEMY

Behind the Rumyantsev garden, in which there is a black granite obelisk commemorating the victory of the Russian army over the Turks, led by Field Marshal Rumyantsev (1768–74), is the **Academy of Fine Arts** ⓬ (Akademiya Khudozhestv). Built by Kokorinov and Vallin de la Mothe between 1764–88, the edifice is considered to be one of the finest examples of 18th-century Russian architecture, and shows the transition from baroque to neo-classical style. It stands out both because of the originality of its location and the artistic wealth of its interior.

Many important Russian painters and sculptors attended this academy, which was founded in 1757, and many of their works are on display in its ★ **Art Museum** (open Wed–Sun 11am–6pm).

Also housed in the academy is the St Petersburg Institute for Painting, Plastics and Architecture, as well as a museum in memory of the famous Ukranian poet and prose writer Taras Shevchenko, who lived and worked here from 1826 until 1834.

Kruzenstern's statue

NAVAL CADET CORPS

Towards the western end of University Embankment is a road to the right – 8 Liniya – along which you will find the **Church of the Annuciation** (Blagoveshenskaya Tserkov, 1765), on the corner of Maly Prospekt. It is a good example of how old Russian building components were used in 18th-century architecture in St Petersburg.

The streets running north to south on Vasilievsky Island are named as and numbered by *liniya* or lines. On the embankment – between the 11 and 13 Liniya – is a residence, formerly belonging to Field Marshal Münnich and later reconstructed by Volkhov in 1796, known as the **Naval Cadet Corps** ⓭ (Morskoy Kadetsky Korpus). In front of the academy on the quay there is a statue of Admiral Kruzenstern, under whose command Russian ships sailed round the world at the beginning of the 19th century. Kruzenstern died in 1846.

MINING INSTITUTE

A bit farther on (corner of Embankment/15 Liniya) is a church that belonged to the town house maintained in St Petersburg by the Kiev Cloister (Kiev Petscherskaya Lavra). It is now used once again as a place of worship. At the end of the quay is the **Mining Institute** ⓮ (Gorny Institut; 1806–8, by Voronichin) with an imposing Doric colonnade.

Below: a street mural of the Lutheran Church
Bottom: the Church of the Annunciation

The massive walls of the building and the two groups of sculptures by Demut-Malinovsky (left: *Attack on Proserpina*, right: *Hercules Fights with Antaeus*) were created to portray man's bond with the earth, and consequently emphasise the purpose of the building. The Institute contains a fine mineral, gem and art collection, which include Fabergé pieces, but it is closed to the public.

LUTHERAN CHURCH

North of the embankment, stretching from east to west, almost parallel, are the Bolshoy (Great), Sredny (Middle) and Maly (Small) Prospekts/ Avenues of Vasilievsky Island, all laid out in the 18th century. Many houses have been retained from that period including the Lutheran **Church of St Catherine** (Bolshoy Prospekt 1, by Velten) with a four-columned portal with bas-reliefs and sculptures in the niches.

Map below

Monument of Peter the Great

2: Great Squares

Decembrists' Square – St Isaac's Square – Palace Square

The Commission for the Development of St Petersburg put forward the idea of building three parade grounds in the city centre in the middle of the 18th century. However, 100 years passed before the ensemble of Decembrists' Square, St Isaac's Square and Palace Square had been completed.

DECEMBRISTS' SQUARE

Ploshchad Dekabristov (Decembrists' Square) was renamed in 1925 in commemoration of the Decembrists' revolt on 14 December 1825. The attractive square, called Senatskaya Ploshchad (Senate Square) in Tsarist times, has a broad view of the River Neva.

In the middle of the square is the famous ★★ **Monument of Peter the Great** ❶❺ (Medny Vsadnik), known as *The Bronze Horseman*. On an

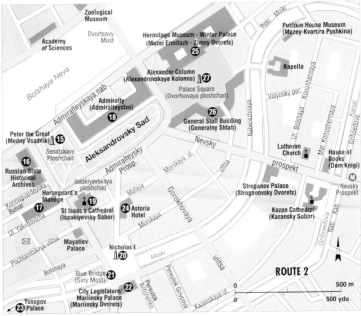

enormous granite base (1,600 tons) shaped like the crest of a wave, Peter I rides a rearing horse. Commissioned by Catherine the Great and designed by Etienne Maurice Falconet, this monument is regarded as one of the most important examples of 18th-century sculpture. It dominates the entire square and underlines the significant role of Peter I in Russian history and the development of the city.

City Archives

To the west, the square is bordered by two cream-coloured buildings, richly decorated with columns and figures. They are linked by an arch which stretches across Galernaya Ulitsa. Within are the **Russian State Historical Archives** (Gosudarstveny Istorichesky Arkhiv). During the days of imperial Russia this was the headquarters of the Senate and the Holy Synod, the highest secular and spiritual institutions after the monarchy. Constructed by Rossi in neoclassical style, they represent his last major work (1834).

Adjoining this building in the north is the neoclassical **Horseguards Manège** ⓱ (Konnogvardeysky Manezh). The building resembles an ancient Greek temple, and was built according to Quarenghi's designs in 1807. The middle section of the columned hall is decorated with a double colonnade and statues of the Dioscuri, sons of Zeus. The statues were prepared in Italy and modelled on the Quirinale Palace in Rome (1817, by Triscorni). This building served for only a short time as a riding school; Johann Strauss gave concerts here in the 19th century, and today it is the Association of Fine Arts' exhibition hall *(see panel, above right)*.

Admiralty

The east side of the square is occupied by the cream-coloured ★★**Admiralty** ⓲ (Admiralteystvo). It was built between 1806 and 1823 by Zacharov on the site once monopolised by the shipyards responsible for launching the first Russian ships during Peter the Great's reign. The

Star Attractions
- Peter the Great Monument
- Admiralty

Art venue
The Manège exhibition hall is now among the city's premier art venues, where leading works by contemporary artists, photographers, sculptors, and performance artists are regularly shown. While outside it is a thoroughly classical structure, inside it is a modern three-floor exhibition hall.

The Senate and Synod from the Embankment

Map on page 34

Admiralty has always been regarded as one of the most beautiful buildings in the city. Now a naval academy, it has also been designated a UNESCO World Heritage Site. The significance of the building as a symbol of the seafaring strength of the country is emphasised by its sculptures.

Over the middle section, the gilded tip of the spire is crowned by a weather vane in the form of a golden sailing ship (total height 72.5m/238ft), the emblem of St Petersburg.

The side of the Admiralty bordering Decembrists' Square measures 163m (535ft), and the facade which stretches from Admiralty Prospekt on Decembrists' Square to Palace Square is 407m (1,335ft) long. Bordered to the south by the Neva, there is a fine view from Decembrists' Square across the river to the right bank and the Peter and Paul Fortress, the Rostral Columns and the University Embankment. From the harbour, riverboats offer a number of interesting excursions along the Neva.

St Isaac's Square

No expense spared
The state did not spare any expense decorating St Isaac's, the most important cathedral of the capital: the total costs incurred were almost 10 times those incurred for the tsar's residence the Winter Palace.

St Isaac's facade

Between Decembrists' Square and St Isaac's Square stands ★★ **St Isaac's Cathedral** ⑲ (Isaak-iyevsky Sobor; open Thur–Tues 11am–6pm, last admission 6pm; Colonnade observation point Thur–Tues 11am–5pm, last admission 4pm; closed Wed). Designed by the French architect Montfer-

rand, the cathedral, with its huge dome, took almost 40 years to construct (1819–58); it is 105.5m (346ft) high, 111.2m (365ft) long, 97.6m (320ft) wide, and can accommodate 14,000 people.

The building is decorated with 112 red granite columns, as well as bronze statues and domes which are covered in over 100kg (220lbs) of pure gold. The exterior walls are clad in grey marble, and inside, in addition to the 14 varieties of marble, many different kinds of natural stones were used, with the result that the cathedral practically doubles as a museum of minerals.

The front entrance is decorated with bronze bas-reliefs depicting biblical themes. On the west side in the lower left-hand corner is a semireposed figure of a man in a toga. It portrays Montferrand holding a model of St Isaac's Cathedral. The interior furnishings – pictures, frescoes, mosaics, windows and in particular the painting on the ceiling of the main dome by Brullov – are all as breathtaking as each other.

In 1931 the cathedral was turned into a museum. Until 1988 the largest Foucault pendulum in the world (weight: 54kg/119lbs, length 93m/305ft) was one of the many pieces on exhibit; however, it was not hung up again after its renovation. This pendulum can be used to show the rotation of the earth.

A visit to the Colonnade observation point at the base of the dome (300 steps) affords a magnificent view of the city.

MYATLEV PALACE

Heading south from the cathedral, on the corner of the Pochtamtskaya Ulitsa, is the square's oldest building, the **Myatlev Palace**, which is thought to have been built by Rinaldi in 1760. The French encyclopaedist and novelist Diderot lived here from 1773 to 1774. Pushkin, a friend of the poet Myatlev, was also a regular guest.

Further towards the Moika is the **statue of Nicholas I** ㉑. The equestrian statue, designed by August Montferrand and executed by Peter von Klodt-Jürgensburg, was cast in 1859. This is

Star Attraction
● St Isaac's Cathedral

Below: the west door of St Isaac's
Bottom: Nicholas I

Map on page 34

Rasputin

Rasputin, peasant, mystic, holy man, had gained a magnetic influence over the empress Alexandra and Tsar Nicholas II, through his apparent ability to ease the bleeding of the haemophiliac crown prince. So powerful did he become that he was seen as a threat to the future of the already war-torn Russian Empire. So a party of noblemen, led by the Grand Duke Dimitry Pavlovich and Prince Yusupov, conspired to eliminate him. On the night of 29–30 December 1916, Rasputin was invited to visit Yusupov's home. He was given poisoned wine and tea cakes, but this didn't kill him. Nor did the two ensuing gunshots. In the end he was bound up and tossed into the icy Neva River, where he drowned.

The Blue Bridge

perhaps the only equestrian statue in Europe that stands on two points (the horse's two hind hooves); others usually stand on three (two hind hooves and the tail). Today, scholars do not understand how Montferrand and Klodt achieved such perfect balance, and so they fear touching and restoring it.

BLUE BRIDGE

The Moika River cuts through St Isaac's Square and is spanned by the **Blue Bridge** ㉑ (Siny Most), which is about 90m (300ft) wide and 35m (115ft) long. Until serfdom was abolished in Russia in 1861, the bridge, which was painted blue at that time, was where serfs were bought and sold. Over the bridge, occupying the former Mariinsky Palace (Mariinsky Dvorets), is the **City Legislature** ㉒. The palace, which was built by Stakenschneider for Maria, the oldest daughter of Nicholas I, now houses the St Petersburg City Council. On the west side of the square is the Institute for Plant Genetics, the Vavilov Institute, and on the east side the Botanical Institute.

YUSUPOV PALACE

Further up the Moika, the long yellow building at No 94 is the ★★ **Yusupov Palace** ㉓ (Yusupovsky Dvorets), built by de la Mothe in the 1760s.

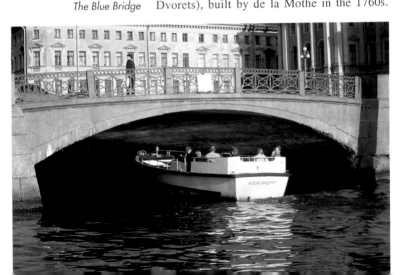

Residence of the wealthy Yusupov family, the palace witnessed one of Russian history's moments of high drama – the murder of Grigory Rasputin.

Visitors can learn about Rasputin, his mysterious life and equally mysterious death from an exhibition in the cellars, but the main draw here is the sumptuous interior of the palace, which includes the exotic Moorish Room, replete with fountain and mosaics (open daily 11am–6pm).

THE ASTORIA

On the corner of the Bolshaya Morskaya Ulitsa is the **Astoria Hotel 24**. With its splendid interiors, the hotel is a fine example of the successful architectural experiments performed in the early 20th century (1912, by Lidval). The leaders of the German Army had planned to hold a reception in the banqueting hall of the Astoria upon capturing the city, and had even printed invitations which were found in Berlin after the war among the remains of the Third Reich's headquarters.

Bolshaya Morskaya Ulitsa runs across both sides of St Isaac's Square. On its southwest side are three noteworthy houses. At No 52 is Polovtsev's House (1835 by Pel) which houses St Petersburg's Architects' Association, and has a beautiful restaurant. Opposite, at No 45, is Princess Gagarina's House (1845 by Montferrand), today the Composers' Association (Dom Kompozitorov).

Next door, No 47 is where the famous emigré writer Vladimir Nabokov, author of Lolita, was born. His house is now home to the offices of the newspaper, *Nevskoe Vremya*, as well as the **Vladimir Nabokov Museum**. There are not many items on display, but a number of the rooms preserve the original interior of the house.

MAIN THOROUGHFARE

From the Astoria Hotel, Bolshaya Morskaya Ulitsa runs northeast. Together with the parallel-running **Malaya Morskaya Ulitsa**, this was once the main thoroughfare of the St Petersburg business district. Large banks, credit and insurance

Star Attraction
● **Yusupov Palace**

Below: the Blue room, at Yusupov Palace
Bottom: the Astoria's banqueting hall

Map on page 34

Fabergé eggs

Carl Fabergé (1846–1920) turned a small family jewellers in St Petersburg into a successful company known throughout the world. In 1884 he was commissioned to create an Easter egg for the empress – the first in a series of imperial eggs exchanged by the tsar and tsarina every year until the Revolution. The *pièce de résistance* is the Siberian Railway Egg, containing a miniature of the royal train.

The sign of Fabergé

companies were based here, an example being the Russian Bank of Trade and Industry (Bolshaya Morskaya Ulitsa 15). Peretyakovich designed this house in 1910 to match the spirit of Russian Classicism using motifs from the Italian Renaissance.

Many of Russia's outstanding creative minds have lived in Malaya Morskaya Ulitsa. Nikolai Gogol lived at No 17 from 1833–6; here he wrote *Dead Souls* and *The Inspector General*. Piotr Tchaikovsky lived and died at No 13. Fiodor Dostoyevsky lived from 1847–9 at No 23 and Alexander Herzen lived at No 25. From 1832–3 Alexander Pushkin lived in No 26, where he worked on his *Dubrovsky*. The most famous Russian jewellers, Fabergé, had their shop at No 24.

PALACE SQUARE

After passing the crossroad (Bolshaya Morskaya Ulitsa with Nevsky Prospekt) and two magnificent triumphal arches, you reach ★★★ **Palace Square** (Dvortsovaya Ploshchad). Although the surrounding buildings reflect very different period styles, the overall effect is of a harmonious whole.

Many events that have had an important effect on the course of Russian history have taken place in this square. It provided the stage for the events that shook the Russian imperium, brought down the imperial throne and heralded the foundation of the Soviet Union.

On 9 January 1905, the day referred to as Bloody Sunday in the history books, 140,000 demonstrators, mainly workers with their families, marched to the Winter Palace with icons, flags and pictures in order to hand a petition to Nicholas II. They were led by Father Gapon, who it was later said was a police spy. The army was waiting for them and opened fire. More than a hundred people were left dying in the snow and many more were wounded. This was the beginning of the 1905 uprising that Lenin described as the dress rehearsal for the October Revolution.

It was again in this square that in February 1917 the tsar's standard was lowered from the flagpole, never to be raised again; later, on 25 October, sections of the Red Guard, as well as service-men sympathetic to the cause, stormed the former imperial palace, in which the Provisional Government and what was left of its loyal troops were hiding. This attack on the Winter Palace, and the capture of members of Kerensky's Provisional Government (Kerensky escaped to the US), marked the beginning of the 1917 Revolution.

Star Attractions
● **Palace Square**
● **Winter Palace**

Below: Catherine the Great
Bottom: the Winter Palace,
side entrance

WINTER PALACE

The entire north side of the square is taken up by the main (south) facade of the ★★★ **Winter Palace** ㉕ (Zimny Dvorets), residence of nearly all the Russian tsars from Peter's daughter Elisabeth to the end of the Romanov dynasty. The palace, for over 200 years the focus of attention for the entire Russian population, is the most magnificent of the Russian palaces. It is the work of the Italian architect Bartolomeo Rastrelli (1700–71). When Rastrelli's father, the sculptor Carlo Rastrelli, was invited by Peter the Great to come to Russia, son followed father, and Bartolomeo subsequently pursued most of his career in St Petersburg.

Work began in 1754, on the request of Elisabeth Petrovna, Peter the Great's daughter, who reigned for 20 years (1741–61). Since the Empress and the architect both shared the same preference for the powerful, slightly Italianate Russian

Map on page 34

Former glory returns
The Winter Palace got its name by acting as the tsars' winter residence, while in the summer they held court in the Catherine Palace in Tsarskoe Selo. The Winter Palace's courtyard was left abandoned and dilapidated in Soviet times, but was reconstructed and reopened in 2001. Concerts are sometimes held here in the summer, and the Hermitage Museum plans to use the courtyard as the main entrance into the museum itself, as opposed to entering from the embankment.

baroque, the palace was festooned with stucco, statues, columned halls and colonnades. Even at the time it was in a baroque world of its own (1,050 rooms, 1,787 windows, 117 staircases), although it was still not complete by the time Elisabeth Petrovna died. Peter III, who only reigned for a few months, was not interested in continuing the work. He was followed by Catherine II who was more interested in Classicism, perhaps because Classicism had just come back into fashion in Paris. She had the work finished and also had the Small Hermitage added by Vallin de la Mothe.

Only the brick facade and the ground floor survived the fire that gutted the palace in 1837; however, just 18 months later Vasily Stasov and Aleksandr Brullov had finished the restoration. On its completion an extravagant gala was held to receive the foreign ambassadors.

The Winter Palace is lavishly decorated with marble, malachite, jasper, bronze, fine wood, rock crystal and gemstones. The **Hermitage Museum** *(see page 87)* opened in 1946 and incorporates many palaces, of which the Winter Palace is the largest. The other palaces are: the Small Hermitage (1764–5, by Vallin de la Mothe), the Old Hermitage (1771–87, by Velten), the Hermitage Theatre (1783–7, by Quarenghi) and the New Hermitage (1839–52, by von Klenze and Stakenschneider).

Monumental sculpture on the Old Hermitage

GENERAL STAFF BUILDING

Opposite the Winter Palace is the old **General Staff Building ㉖** (Glavny Shtab) and **Ministry for Foreign Affairs**. They were built between 1820–45 by Carlo Rossi and together form a semicircle. Linking the two is a double triumphal arch, which was erected to commemorate victory over Napoleon's troops; as was the victory chariot, by Vasily Demut-Malinovsky and Stepan Pimyenov, crowning the arch.

The former Guard Corps Headquarters borders the east side of the square. The facade of this complex links the buildings by Rastrelli (Winter Palace) and Rossi (General Staff Building). At the end of October 1917 the defence corps followed

Lenin's instructions to defend the city against the attack of General Kornilov's anti-revolutionary troops. A plaque commemorating this hangs in the south entrance.

To the west can be seen one side of the Admiralty overlooking the Decembrists' Square, as well as the **Admiralteysky Sad** (Admiralty Garden), which runs parallel to Admiralty Prospekt. In the garden, which dates from 1845, are busts of Gogol, Lermontov, Glinka and other famous names in Russian history.

Where the Palace and Admiralty Embankments meet – between the east side of the Admiralty and the west facade of the Winter Palace – the Palace Bridge (Dvortsovy Most) joins the Neva Embankment with the eastern tip of Vasilievsky Island.

COLOSSAL COLUMN

In the middle of Palace Square stands the 47.5m (156ft) ★ **Alexander Column** ㉗ (Aleksandrovskaya Kolonna). This colossal monolith of pink granite was erected in 1830–34 by Auguste Montferrand, and is dedicated to Tsar Alexander I for his role in Russia's truimph over Napoleon (*see pages 16–17*). Crowning the column is a gilded angel in the likeness of the tsar. Weighing 600 tonnes, the column is the largest free-standing monument in the world.

Below: the Alexander Column
Bottom: the side of the General Staff Building

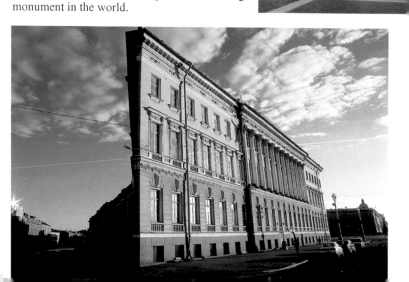

Map on page 45

Street of tolerance

In tsarist times, Nevsky Prospekt was nicknamed the 'street of religious toleration' because of the great number of churches of varying Christian denominations in such a short distance. Among them were and still are Catholic, Armenian, Lutheran, and Dutch Reformed. Only the last was not reopened after the Soviet era.

The wartime artillery warning

3: Nevsky Prospekt

In 1710 a path was cut through the trees in the southeastern section of the Neva Embankment. Transformed into a magnificent avenue, this path, first known as the Great Perspective Road, later took on the name of Nevsky Prospekt, after Alexander Nevsky (1220–63), the prince of Novgorod who defeated the Swedes in 1240 and was later canonised. His remains were transferred to the Alexander Nevsky Monastery *(see page 72)*, situated at the end of Nevsky Prospekt.

STREET OF VARIETY

During the 19th century some of the period's most famous architects were responsible for creating the symmetrical shapes of the buildings. Between 25–60m (82–197ft) wide, the avenue stretches in a straight line for 2.5km (1½ miles), from the centre tower of the Admiralty *(see page 35)* to Vosstaniya Ploshchad or Uprising Square (at one point known as Znamenskaya Ploshchad). From here, after a gentle right turn, it is another 2km (1 mile) to the Alexander Nevsky Monastery.

Along Nevsky Prospekt there are many museums, offices, companies, restaurants, theatres and cinemas. People come here to work, shop, sit in a café or just to wander around. Nevsky Prospekt is the equivalent to London's Oxford Street or Paris's Champs-Elysées. The most interesting section of this delightful avenue lies between the Admiralty and the Fontanka River. Almost every one of these houses has experienced something of St Petersburg's history.

FINE HOUSES

All the buildings down to Vosstaniya Ploshchad were built before 1917 except for the secondary school (No 14). At the beginning of the Prospekt, just behind the Admiralty, are the buildings that came into being at the turn of the 20th century. These include, for example, the St Petersburg

Trade Bank (Nos 7/9), or Palace of the Wollenberg bankers as it is often called, for which Peretyatkovitch used motives from the Venetian Renaissance (today it houses the Aeroflot office).

Outside the secondary school (No 14), the only new building (1939) in this section of Nevsky Prospekt, there is still a plaque dating from World War II bearing the message: 'Citizens! During artillery fire this side of the street is more dangerous.'

Nevsky Prospekt at the beginning of the 20th century

On the right-hand (i.e. south) side of Nevsky Prospekt, between Bolshaya Morskaya Ulitsa and Moika Embankment (Naberezhnaya Moiki), is one of the city's oldest houses at **No 15 ㉘**. It was built by Kokorinov in 1771 on the same spot occupied by the temporary wooden palace of Empress Yelisaveta Petrovna (Elisabeth I) from 1765–8.

On the other side of Nevsky Prospekt, No 18 used to be the **Wulf and Béranger Café**, popular with St Petersburg's litterati. It was from here, on 27 February 1837, that Pushkin met his companion and then rode to his duel with D'Anthès, in which he was mortally wounded.

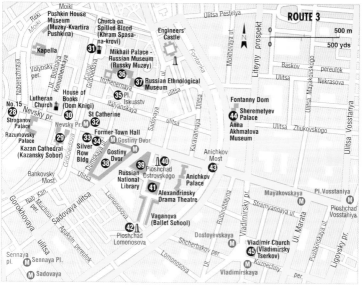

Below: a statue outside the
Razumovsky Palace
Bottom: Kazan Cathedral steps

The land behind the Moika River on the left (i.e. north) side of the Prospekt used to be reserved for non-Orthodox churches. The first one is the former Dutch Church (Gollandskaya Tserkov, No 20), embellished with a shallow dome and projecting, Classical portico. It was built in 1836 and Jacquot modelled it on the tomb of Diocletian in Split, Croatia.

STROGANOV PALACE

On the other side of the road is a light red building with white columns. It is the ★ **Stroganov Palace** (Stroganovsky Dvorets, 1754, by Rastrelli), one of the most famous monuments to Russian baroque in this avenue. The sculptures at the main entrance, which represent sphinxes, were added at the end of the 18th century by the architect Voronikhin whilst he was restoring the palace. He had been Count Stroganov's servant during his youth and had lived in the palace. Today, part of the collection from the Russian Museum is housed here.

On the embankment next to the Stroganov Palace is the former **Razumovsky Palace** (Dvorets Razumovskogo), built by Kokorinov and de la Mothe in 1766, and now the home of the Pedagogical Institute (Naberezhnaya Moiki 48).

On the left-hand (north) side of Nevsky Prospekt take a look at the symmetrical form of architecture used for houses Nos 22 and 24. Between them stands the former Lutheran **Church of St Peter**, built in Romanesque style (1838, by Bryullov). In Soviet times it housed a swimming pool, but was returned to the Lutheran Church in the mid-1990s.

KAZAN CATHEDRAL

Nevsky Prospekt continues east to Kazan Square (Kazanskaya Ploshchad), dominated by the ★★ **Kazan Cathedral** ㉙ (Kazansky Sobor, also known as the Cathedral of Our Lady of Kazan), the most beautiful edifice on Nevsky Prospekt. Designed by Voronikhin and modelled on St

Peter's in Rome, the cathedral was built between 1801–11. It is surmounted by an enormous 90m-high (295ft) dome. For the construction of the cathedral cast-iron supports were used for the first time. The most distinguishing feature of the building is the magnificent semicircular colonnade, made up of 96 Corinthian columns hewn from Karelian granite. The graceful effect of the exterior is mirrored by the 56 columns inside, which are crowned by bronze capitals.

Standing in the niches of the porticoes overlooking Nevsky Prospekt are bronze statues of Prince Vladimir, Alexander Nevsky, St Andrew and St John the Baptist. Enormous biblical reliefs decorate both ends of the building.

The cathedral is also a memorial to the victory won in the war of 1812. To the right of the entrance, it is possible to see the grave and bust of the old Field Marshal Kutuzov who, history records, collected himself here before leading the decisive battle of Smolensk.

By the beginning of the 20th century, a kind of military museum had been installed in the cathedral to exhibit all the trophies captured from Napoleon's army after it was defeated in the snow of White Russia. There are also the keys to the 28 cities captured during the campaign, including Hamburg, Dresden, Leipzig, Reims and Utrecht. It is still possible to view these trophies.

Star Attraction
● **Kazan Cathedral**

Moving collection
From 1932 to 2000, Kazan Cathedral housed the Museum of Atheism and Religion, but in accordance with current state policy to return churches back to their original function, the museum has since been moved to a location near the Central Post Office on Pochshtamskaya Ulitsa. With one of the largest collections of religious artefacts in the world, from ancient pagan times to the 20th century, the museum makes an interesting detour.

Kazan Cathedral and fountain at night

Map on page 45

HOUSE OF THE BOOK

Opposite the cathedral at No 28 is the **House of the Book ㉚** (Dom Knigi). Constructed between 1902–4 by Suzor for the Singer Sewing Machine Company, the building, whose glass tower supports a huge globe, now houses the largest bookshop in the city and a series of publishing houses.

Below: mosaic detail on (bottom) Church on the Spilled Blood

CHURCH ON THE SPILLED BLOOD

Immediately behind Kazan Square flows the Yekaterinsky Canal. Cross the Kazan Bridge (Kazansky Most), built by Golenitsev Kutuzov (father of the great commander) in 1766, and considerably widened in 1805. To the left (i.e. north) of the bridge on the right-hand side of the Ekaterinsky Canal, past the Mikhail Palace *(see page 50)*, is the astoundingly beautiful **★★★ Church on the Spilled Blood ㉛** (Khram Spasa-na-Krovi, open 11am–6pm; closed Wed), also known as the Cathedral of the Resurrection of Christ (Khram Voskreseniya Khristova). Designed by Makarow and Parland, the church was built between 1883–1907 on the spot where Alexander II was assassinated by members of the Narodnaya Volya terrorist organisation in 1881.

The church's architecture contains elements reflecting traditional 17th-century Russian style

– particularly reminiscent of Moscow's St Basil's Cathedral. However, Kiev's Vladimir Cathedral can be seen to have influenced the design of the dome. The facade and the interior are decorated with exquisite mosaics.

BACK ON NEVSKY PROSPEKT

On the other side of the bridge on the left-hand side of Nevsky Prospekt, house No 30 is of interest. Concerts were held here by the Philharmonic Orchestra (founded in 1802), at which not only the best Russian musicians but also guest composers such as Berlioz, Wagner, Johann Strauss and Liszt took part. Today the Glinka Hall is used by the St Petersburg Philharmonic Orchestra.

At Nos 32/4 of Nevsky Prospekt stands the **Catholic Church of St Catherine ㉜**. Its facade reflects the architectural transition from baroque to Classicism.

Farther along, on the corner of Nevsky Prospekt/ Mikhailovskaya Ulitsa and past the interesting **Silver Row (Serebryanny Ryady) Building ㉝**, is the former **Town Hall ㉞** (Gorodskaya Duma) with its triple-tiered red tower. The town councillors hold their meetings here, in what was originally planned as a concert hall.

Standing alone next to the old Town Hall, the **Portik Rusca**, an elegant Classical portico, was originally the entrance to a long arcade of shops (1806, by Ruska). The portico was dismantled during the construction of the metro and rebuilt in 1972. Today, it houses the city's theatre box office (*teatralnaya kassa*).

PLOSHCHAD ISKUSSTV

Opposite the Town Hall, the short Mikhailovskaya Ulitsa turns off left from the Prospekt. It leads to the architectural ensemble of ★★ **Ploshchad Iskusstv ㉟** (the Square of the Arts). The design for the street and square was drawn up by the architect Carlo Rossi.

The south side of the square is bordered on the left by one of Russia's most famous hotels, the

Star Attractions
● **Church on the Spilled Blood**
● **Ploshchad Iskusstv**

Multi-purpose tower
The town hall tower used to signal dangers such as fires and floods; later it became one of the telegraph stations between the Winter Palace and the Summer Residence in Tsarskoe Selo.

The Grand Hotel Europe

Map on page 45

Shostakovitch
On 9 August 1942, during the desperate days of the blockade, Dmitri Shostakovitch's 7th (Leningrad) Symphony, which he composed in the besieged city, was performed by a group of surviving musicians as an act of defiance on the very day that Hitler had decreed that the city should fall. He had started work on the symphony within a month of the German invasion of the Soviet Union in 1941, and it became a beacon of anti-Nazi resistance.

ornate **Grand Hotel Europe**, whose art nouveau restaurant (by Livdal) was a favourite rendezvous for members of the diplomatic corps and secret police before the Revolution, and in the 1970s became a popular meeting place for young intellectuals and artists.

On the right stands what was, until the Revolution, the Noble Assembly (1834–9 by Jacquot), a little like the British House of Lords. Today it is the main **Shostakovitch Hall** of the St Petersburg Philharmonic Orchestra; entrance Mikhailovskaya Ulitsa 2. Many top soloists have played here, as well as top conductors of the calibre of Karajan, Ferrero, etc. The St Petersburg Philharmonic Orchestra, which has performed in most of the major cities of Europe, is regarded as one of the best orchestras in the world.

MIKHAIL PALACE

The northern side of Ploshchad Iskusstv is bordered by the magnificent building of the former ★★★ **Mikhail Palace** ㊱ (Mikhailovsky Dvorets), built by Rossi in Classical style between 1819–25 for the Grand Duke Mikhail, the younger brother of Alexander I and Nicholas I. The main facade of the palace is decorated with 20 pillars and a frieze consisting of 44 bas-reliefs. On both sides of the wide staircases are bronze lions. The wrought-iron railing separating the front courtyard from the square is one of the best examples of its kind in the city.

After the Grand Duke's death his widow, the Grand Duchess Helene, turned the magnificent building into a meeting place for educated nobles and the greatest artists of the day. The musical soirées organised by Anton Rubinstein – who engaged the best-known European interpreters – were celebrated here. After the death of the Grand Duchess in 1873 and then that of her daughter, the state bought back the palace.

The ★★★ **Russian Museum** (Russky Muzey, open Wed–Mon 10am–6pm; closed Tues) was opened in the Mikhail Palace in 1898, and substantial renovations were completed in time for

The Pushkin statue, Ploshchad Iskusstv

the centennial celebrations. It is the world's largest museum of Russian art, containing more than 400,000 works from the fine arts, including many paintings and sculptures.

The collection ranges from medieval Russian icons to modern art. In the west wing of the museum, which overlooks the Griboyedov Canal, there are paintings from the Soviet Period.

Star Attractions
● **Mikhail Palace**
● **Russian Museum**

Below: an icon and (bottom) the Grand Staircase of the Russian Museum

RUSSIAN ETHNOLOGICAL MUSEUM

Adjoining the east side of the building (Inzhenyernaya Ulitsa 4) is the **Russian Ethnological Museum** ❼ (Muzey Etnografii; open Tues–Sun 11am–6pm; closed Mon). This spacious museum comprises a series of rooms set out in parallel arrangement. Virtually every ethnic group of the old Soviet Empire is represented here – from the Baltic people to the Steppe people of Manchuria; from the Laplanders and tribes from the Polar region to nomadic tribes from the Muslim and Eastern population east of the Black Sea; from the White Russians to the inhabitants of remotest Siberia; from the Moldavians and Ukranians to the Armenians and beyond.

Reconstructions of house interiors and dioramas of native village life paint a picture of the differences between the lifestyles of the ethnic groups. Their arts and crafts are also highlighted.

Below: a puppet theatre sign,
Nevsky Prospekt
Bottom: the Armenian Church
and trolley bus

THEATRES AND MUSEUMS

The west side of the square is bordered by the
house which was formerly the French Comedy
Theatre, built by Bryullov in 1833 (facade by
Rossi). Since 1918 it has been the home of the
Maly Theatre, the city's main ballet and opera
house after the venerable Mariinsky *(see page 76)*.
Next door (No 3) is the **Brodsky Museum**. Isaak
Brodsky (1884–1939) was one of the best known
painters of his day.

In a green enclosure in the middle of Ploshchad
Iskusstv is a statue of Pushkin reciting his poetry,
by the city's leading postwar sculptor, Anikushin
(1957). Bordering Italyanskaya Ulitsa on the
southern-side of the square (No 13) is the **Theatre
for Musical Comedies** (the so-called Blockade
Theatre) and the **Komissarzhevsky Theatre**
(Komissarzhevsky Theatre, No 19), whose first
production was staged on 18 October 1942.

GOSTINY DVOR

Stretching over 280m (920ft) along Nevsky
Prospekt from the Town Hall to the Sadovaya
Ulitsa is the building of **Gostiny Dvor** ❸, St
Petersburg's largest department store (similar to
GUM in Moscow). Measuring over 1km (½ mile)
in circumference and housing 300-odd shops, this
enormous two-storey building was a centre of

commerce, deriving its name from the Old Russian word, 'gost', which means merchant.

On the opposite side of the Prospekt between houses Nos 40 and 42 (slightly set back from the street) is the light blue neoclassical building of the **Armenian Church** (1772, by Velten), which reopened in August 1993. A bit further on at No 48 is the **Passage**, a two-storey shopping arcade.

Beyond Sadovaya Ulitsa, three houses further on at the junction of Nevsky Prospekt and Malaya Sadovaya Ulitsa, stands house No 56, erected in 1907 as the premises of the merchant Yeliseyev, and lavishly decorated in the art nouveau style by architect Baranovsky. Today it is one of the biggest food stores in St Petersburg, though it still retains its original elegance. On the top floor is St Petersburg's **Comedy Theatre** (Teatr Komedii).

RUSSIAN NATIONAL LIBRARY

On the other side of the street (No 18) stands the ★ **Russian National Library** ③⑨ (not open to the public). Founded in 1814, it is today the second largest library in the country, with over 20 million books. These include samples of Peter I's handwriting, the largest collection of incunabula in the world, and the 7,000-volume library Voltaire presented to Catherine II. The imposing building, which was built by Sokolov in 1794 to house a library, had to be extended by Rossi. The 18-columned main entrance borders one side of Ploshchad Ostrovskovo. It was on the Prospekt opposite the library that government troops shot at demonstrators on 4 July 1917.

STATUE OF CATHERINE II

Ploshchad Ostrovskovo ④⓪ (Ostrovsky Square) opens out to the right of Nevsky Prospekt. The architectural unity of the square (1828) is one of Rossi's finest accomplishments. In a small garden in the middle of the square is a 4-m (13-ft) **statue of the Empress Catherine II,** surrounded by bronze figures portraying – in vivid likeness – some of the principal personalities who lived in Russia

> **Foiled attempt**
> Since the collapse of the Soviet Union, the Russian National Library has been targeted many times by thieves, with the most spectacular heist taking place in December 1994 when a group of thieves tried to steal 47 medieval European and 45 ancient Chinese, Mongolian, Tibetan, and Hebrew manuscripts, worth about $300 million, and sell them to a collector in Israel. A joint operation by Russian and Israeli police rounded up the culprits, and the scrolls were recovered.

Gostiny Dvor shopping arcade at night

Map on page 45

Below: the Aleksandrinsky Theatre
Bottom: Lomonosov Square

in the second half of the 18th-century, including Orlov, Potemkin, Derzhavin and Rumyantsev.

Behind the monument at the back of the square stands the **Pushkin Drama Theatre ㊶**, still known as the Aleksandrinsky. The theatre, designed by Carlo Rossi, was erected between 1828–32. On the Nevsky Prospekt side of the building, an impressive colonnade consisting of six Corinthian columns adorns the theatre facade. The pediment is surmounted by the chariot of the leader of the Muses: Apollo.

ROSSI STREET

Behind the theatre is ★★★**Ulitsa Zodchi Carlo Rossi** (Architect Carlo Rossi Street), named after the architect whom St Petersburg has to thank for so many of its magnificent buildings. This street is in itself a unique contribution to the design of the city. It is perfectly proportioned (220m/720ft long, 22m/72ft wide and with a building height of 22m/72ft). The enormous windows of the facades, alternately paired off with semicircular white columns, make it one of the most beautiful streets in St Petersburg.

The building on the corner of Ulitsa Rossi and Ploshchad Ostrovskovo houses the Theatre and Music Museum, the Committee for Architecture and Town Planning and the Vaganova Ballet

School, where famous dancers such as Pavlova, Nijinsky, and later Nureyev and Makarova trained. The **Theatre Museum** (Teatralny Muzey, open Thur–Mon 10.30am–6pm, Wed 10.30am–1pm; closed Tues) records the history of Russian theatre and has a photo and record collection, which makes it possible to hear the voices of great singers and actors, as well as the works of Russian and foreign dramatists. In addition, there are manuscripts, models, drawings, sketches, and instructions concerning scenery.

LOMONOSOV SQUARE

Ulitsa Rossi leads into ★**Ploshchad Lomonosova** ㊷ (Lomonosov Square), another of Rossi's creations. In the centre of the square is a monument to Lomonosov (1892, by Sabello). Here the facade of the Bolshoy Drama Theatre stretches to the Fontanka Embankment. The house was built from 1831–3 by the architect Bryullov; the facade was Rossi's design.

ANICHKOV PALACE

Behind a beautiful wrought-iron railing on the eastern side of Ploshchad Ostrovskovo, shaded by the trees of a spacious garden, there is another fine example of Russian architecture, the ★**Anichkov Palace**, constructed between 1741–50 and frequently converted since then. The first main facade of the palace, commissioned by Empress Elisabeth for her favourite, Count Razumovsky, overlooked the Fontanka River, since at that time Nevsky Prospekt was not yet the main boulevard of the city. The main entrance was reached by boat. At the beginning of the 19th century, Quarenghi added the monumental building which became the cabinet – the palace chancellery – which blocked the view of the river.

Behind the Anichkov Palace, the ★**Anichkov Bridge** ㊸ (Anitchkov Most) crosses over the Fontanka. It is described as one of the most beautiful bridges in St Petersburg. In 1841 four bronze groups known as *The Horse Tamers* were set up

Romantic overtures
As a boy, Tsar Nicholas II, along with his parents and siblings, spent their winters primarily in the Anichkov Palace, and spent less time in the Winter Palace. It was here, during his walks in the palace gardens, that the young Nicholas II would often watch the beautiful ballerina, Matilda Kshisinskaya, then a student at the nearby Imperial Ballet Academy (now the Vaganova Ballet Academy on Carlo Rossi Street), pass by to and from lessons. The two eventually had a romance that is still talked about today.

One of the Horse Tamers *on Anichkov Bridge*

Map
on page
45

on the bridge in pairs. In 1843 two of these sculptures were sent to Berlin as a present to the Prussian king; in 1846 two others were sent to the king of Naples. In 1850 Klodt made new bronze casts to replace them and these can still be seen on the bridge today. Opposite the Anichkov Palace is another beautiful palace at No 41, built by Stakenschneider between 1846–8 for Prince Beloselsky-Belozersky.

ANNA AKHMATOVA MUSEUM

On the opposite embankment of the river (on the left-hand side of the Prospekt) is a further architectural monument (house No 34), the former Sheremetyev Palace (1755, by Chevakinsky and Argunov). The palace's semicircular parade ground is separated from the embankment by a cast-iron railing, bearing the gilded crest of the Sheremetyev family. Today the **Anna Akhmatova Museum** 44 (open Tues–Sun 10.30am–5.30pm), which describes the life of the famous poetess who suffered under the rule of Stalin (*see box*), is housed in one of the wings of the so-called 'Fontanny Dom'. The Musical Instruments Museum is also housed here.

Anna Akhmatova

Born Anna Andreyevna Gorenko in 1889, Anna Akhmatova, as she came to be known, is generally considered to be the finest woman poet of Russian literature. Associated with the 'Acemsist' group of poets (who espoused clarity in their works), her output is dominated by love poems. Her first (ex-) husband, also a poet, was executed by the Bolsheviks in 1921, and she encountered hostility from the Soviet regime throughout the rest of her life.

Natan Altman's portrait of Anna Akhamatova, 1914

VLADIMIR CHURCH

Nevsky Prospekt then crosses the Liteyny Prospekt (leading off north to the Neva) and the Vladimirsky Prospekt (travelling south). The latter comes to an end in front of the ★ **Vladimir Church** 45 on Vladimirskaya Ploshchad, a magnificent monument to Russian architecture from the 18th century, with its impressive bell tower and five domes. Nearby, in Kuznechny Pereulok, is the lavish **Kuznechny vegetable market** (Tues–Sun 9am–7pm; closed Mon).

Finally, Nevsky Prospekt leads into Vosstaniya Ploshchad (*see page 71*). On the right side of the square is Moscow Station (Moskovsky Vokzal), first built in 1851 and then rebuilt 100 years later. On the left is the metro station and the Oktyabrskaya Hotel.

4: Millionaires' Street

Palace Square – Field of Mars – Summer Garden – Mikhailovsky Castle

Map below

Lined by what were once manor houses, ★ **Millionnaya Ulitsa** (Millionaires' Street) is one of the oldest and most aristocratic streets in St Petersburg. From Palace Square it runs in a northeasterly direction.

Star Attraction
● Winter Canal

WINTER CANAL

On the left is the New Hermitage (*see page 87*), its entrance adorned with 10 giant Atlantes designed by Terebenyev. Millionnaya Ulitsa cuts through the so-called ★★ **Winter Canal** (Zimnaya Kanavka), which links the Moika and Neva rivers and is crossed by three bridges. Of particular interest beyond the canal, at the far end of Millionnaya Ulitsa, on the right at No 4 (corner of Apothecary Lane/Aptekarsky Pereulok), is the building that used to house the court apothecary, erected by Quarenghi between 1789–96.

The Winter Canal

Here, between the Dvortsovaya Naberezhnaya (Palace Embankment) and the Moika are many palaces formerly owned by court dignitaries. The **House of Scholars ㊻** (Dom Uchyenich), at No 26 Dvortsovaya Naberezhnaya, was designed by Rezanov for Alexander II's son Vladimir, president

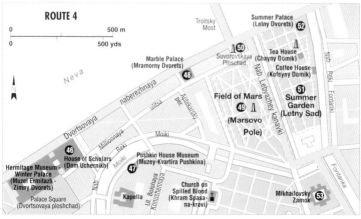

ROUTE 4

0   500 m
0   500 yds

Neva

Troitsky Most

Summer Palace (Letny Dvorets) ㊾

Marble Palace (Mramorny Dvorets)

Suvorovskaya Ploschad ㊿

Tea House (Chayny Domik)

Coffee House (Kofeyny Domik)

Nab. Lebyazhey Kanavki

Nab. Reki Fontanki

naberezhnaya

Aptekarsky per.

Field of Mars ㊸ (Marsovo Pole)

Summer Garden (Letny Sad) ㊱

Dvortsovaya

Millionnaya ulitsa

Moiki

Reki Moiki

Pushkin House Museum (Muzey-Kvartira Pushkina) ㊷

House of Scholars (Dom Uchernikh) ㊻

Hermitage Museum - Winter Palace (Muzei Ermitazh - Zimny Dvorets)

Palace Square (Dvortsovaya ploshchad)

Kapella

Ul. Bolshaya Konyushennaya

Church on Spilled Blood (Khram Spasa-na-krovi)

Fontanka

Mikhailovsky Zamok ㊼

Map on page 57

of the Academy of Arts and commander of the Guards' Troops, who gave the order to shoot on Bloody Sunday in January 1905. Its impressive facade and the well-preserved interior, completed in various styles, are characteristic of Russian architecture from the second half of the 19th century.

Grand Duke Nikolai Mikhailovich's Palace (or former palace), north of Millionnaya Ulitsa at Dvortsovaya Naberezhnaya (No 18), was built by the architect Stakenschneider in rococo style in 1863. No 16 is the old English Club, so frequently mentioned in Tolstoy's *Anna Karenina*; No 14 once housed the similar New Club.

Below: Pushkin's study
Bottom: Millionaires' Street

PUSHKIN MUSEUM

Not far from Millionnaya Ulitsa at Moika Embankment No 12 is the ★ **Pushkin House Museum** ㊼ (Pushkinsky Dom; open Wed–Mon 10.30am–5.30pm; closed Tues). It was here that Pushkin completed his story, *The Captain's Daughter*; he also wrote the history of Peter the Great and composed the poem, *The Bronze Horseman*.

After having been mortally wounded in a duel, the poet spent his last hours in this house. He died on 29 January 1837. Poets come here from all over the world on the anniversary of Pushkin's death to read their newest poems to poetry fans gathered around the memorial in the courtyard.

MARBLE PALACE

At the end of the Millionnaya Ulitsa on the left (house Nos 5–1) is the **★★ Marble Palace** (Wed–Sun 10am–6pm, Mon 10am–5pm; closed Tues). Designed by Rinaldi between 1768–85, the building was commissioned by Catherine II for her favourite, Grigory Orlov, who died before its completion. It later belonged to Grand Duke Konstantin Konstantinovich Romanov.

Deriving its name from its exterior's granite and marble layers, this is one of the finest monuments to early Russian Classicism. During the Soviet era it was home to the Lenin Central Museum; today it is part of the Russian Museum and home to its **Modern Art** department, which concentrates on modern Russian and some Western art from the early 20th century onwards, and puts on some excellent temporary exhibitions.

Star Attraction
● Marble Palace

Form and function
Though it is called the Marble Palace, in fact only the facade is made of marble sheets. The main structure is made of brick. Besides providing display space for modern art, the palace can also be rented for private and public events, and everything from fashion shows to weddings can be held here, for a price of course.

FIELD OF MARS

On the right-hand side of Millionnaya Ulitsa are the old barracks of the Pavlov Guards. This vast building was erected between 1817–21 and designed by Stasov. In February 1917, soldiers from this regiment were among the first to join the insurgent masses. In October 1917 they took part in the storming of the Winter Palace. The main facade overlooks the **★ Field of Mars** (Marsovo Pole) – a square that, in accordance with ancient Roman tradition, received the name because its main function was as a parade ground; troop inspections also took place here.

At the beginning of 1917 the Field of Mars provided the stage for mass demonstrations. After hundreds of workers and soldiers were killed or wounded during the February Revolution, the dead were subsequently buried in a mass grave in the middle of the square. Later, the dead from the October Revolution, the civil war and a number of important people from the communist party were also laid to rest here beneath the flowerbed.

In 1919 the monument commemorating the *Fighters for the Revolution* was unveiled. In 1957 an eternal flame was lit in the middle of the

The Marble Palace at night

Map on page 57

monument, from which the grave of the unknown soldier in Moscow was subsequently lit.

SUVOROV SQUARE

Leading onto this square in the north is the small ★**Ploshchad Suvorova** ❺⓿ (Suvorov Square), where there is a statue to the Russian General Suvorov (1729–1800), a leading character in the Seven Year War, who crushed Pugachev's rebellion and fought the Turks. The sculptor Kozlovsky has portrayed him as a Classical warrior.

To the east of the monument, at the Palace Embankment 4, is the former **Count Saltykov Palace**, built in the Classical style by Quarenghi (1788). At the beginning of the 1830s, the owner of the Count Saltykov Palace, a daughter of Field Marshal Kutuzov, hosted roaring parties here, to which literary figures and politicians were invited.

The facade of the building has remained as Quarenghi designed it in 1784; the interior of the building, however, was completely renovated in 1818. From 1863 until 1918 the building housed the British Embassy.

Suvorov the suppressor

Though considered to be one of Russia's great military leaders and acclaimed a national hero, Suvorov led government troops in the brutal crushing of the peasant uprising in 1774, known to history as Pugachev's Rebellion, when Russian serfs fought against their servitude to the aristocracy. Government troops under Suvorov's command were also called in to suppress the Polish uprising of 1794, when Poles, who had recently been absorbed into the Russian Empire, unsuccessfully fought back for their freedom.

SUMMER GARDEN

To the south of the Field of Mars it is possible to see the rear of the Russian Museum; to the east

The eternal flame on the Field of Mars

flows the Lebyazhy Kanavka (Swan Canal). Since 1715 it has linked the Moika to the Neva. Originally swans nested here, hence the name.

The canal divides the Field of Mars from the famous ★★ **Summer Garden** ⑤ (Letny Sad) to the east, popular with the people of St Petersburg looking for relaxation. In the oldest part of the city, the Summer Garden was laid out between 1704–12 on the initiative of Peter I by landscape gardeners Roosen and Surmin. The garden was planned for the summer residence of the royal family, and the tsar spared no expense in making it as beautiful as possible.

Most of the marble statues were designed by leading Italian masters. A total of 89 statues still line the avenues today. The *Peace and Plenty* monument deserves special attention. It was ordered by Peter I from the Venetian sculptor Baratto in 1722 and symbolises the Nystad Peace Treaty, signed with the defeated Swedes after the Great Northern War. Peter I also commissioned the statues *Architecture* and *Navigation*, an allegory representing the significance of the fleet and the development of St Petersburg.

In the 18th century the statues of Alexander the Great, Julius Caeser, Nero and Claudius were also erected. With the Summer Garden Peter I wanted to create his own Versailles. His court subjects were expected to attend the parties arranged here, together with their wives and daughters, whether it was convenient for them or not.

Today, the original arrangement of the park is only visible on old engravings. Between the canals, which were supposed to be reminiscent of Venice, stood rare trees and valuable statues, brought over from Italy. The conservatories, ponds, cages of rare birds, fountains, labyrinths and rare flowers were the pride of the tsar.

MARBLE STATUES

The park is no less beautiful today. The **marble statues** Peter the Great selected for the Summer Garden, moved around before World II, were put back exactly where the tsar had originally placed

Star Attraction
● Summer Garden

Below: the Summer Garden
Bottom: renovation of the marble statues

Map on page 57

them. During the reign of Peter the Great, only invited guests from the upper classes were allowed to visit the garden. Even after his death, entrance was limited to small groups until the end of the 19th century. At the end of the 18th century its access to the River Neva was shut off by a cast-iron railing (designed by Velten and Yegorov).

On the eastern side of the central avenue is a monument (1855 by Klodt) to the fabulist Ivan Krylov (1768–1844), whose works were translated into over 50 languages. Krylov, the Aesop of Russian literature, loved to go walking in this garden and often met with Pushkin here. Decorating the pedestal of his monument are reliefs depicting various animal characters from his marvellous fables.

Finding perfection

It is said that at the beginning of the 19th century the yacht of an English lord and patron sailed into the Neva and lowered anchor in front of the Summer Garden. The lord, known as an admirer of everything beautiful, studied the railing from the deck of his ship for a few hours, without going ashore, and then ordered the crew to draw anchor. He explained that he had reached the goal of his trip. It would not be possible to surpass such beauty.

SUMMER PALACE

On the Fontanka Embankment, bordering the eastern side of the garden, is the ★ **Summer Palace** 52 (Letny Dvorets Petra), built for Peter the Great by Trezzini. This was the first imperial palace in the new city, and is now open as a museum (open Wed–Mon 10.30am–5pm; closed Tues).

Outside, the building is decorated with bas-reliefs glorifying the victories of the Russian fleet. Inside, each of the two floors of this modest, Dutch-style house has six rooms: Peter I

Romany children in the Summer Garden

lived on the ground floor and his wife Catherine I lived on the first floor. The interior furnishings of the palace, such as the wood carvings in the anteroom, the arrangement of the tsar's study and the empress's green cabinet, the tiled stove in the kitchen and lounge, the paintings on the ceilings (including one in the bedroom showing the triumph of Morpheus, the god of sleep), the tsar's wood-turning lathes, as well as many other personal items have all been preserved. Hence the palace's interior reveals a great deal about Peter the Great's character and his penchant for art and crafts.

The interior looks like one of those bourgeois Amsterdam houses one sees in Vermeer's paintings. The faïence tiles of the big oven as well as a barometer from Amsterdam and a heavy cupboard are all reminiscent of the Dutch town in which Peter the Great worked. The view over the canals with the cloud-covered skies and the large river nearby underline this impression.

To the south of the palace there are two pavilions in the garden: the first, the **Coffee House** (Kofeyny Domik) came into being during the renovation of Peter's Grotto (Rossi), and the second, the **Tea House** (Chayny Domik) was designed by Charlemagne in 1827. The latter, a simple neoclassical pavilion, is now a gallery where it is possible to relax and drink a cup of coffee.

MIKHAILOVSKY CASTLE

At the other side of the Moika – the southern border of the Summer Garden – is Sadovaya Ulitsa, which stretches to the Nevsky Prospekt. On the right is the Mikhailovsky Garden, designed with Rossi's participation in the 19th century.

On the left is ★★**Mikhailovsky Castle** ⑬ (also known as Engineering Castle). It is worth taking a stroll round the outside of this castle, built for Tsar Paul I at the end of the 18th century, since the design of each side was made to match the surrounding countryside. Hence, for example, the north side overlooking the garden is more beautiful than the south side which, over-

Star Attraction
● **Mikhailovsky Castle**

The Mikhailovsky Castle

Map on page 57

Grand Master
In 1799, Paul I made himself Grand Master of the Knights of Malta, at the urging of those European knights living in St Petersburg after Napoleon had conquered the island of Malta and disbanded the Order. Until Paul's death, St Petersburg took on the air of a Maltese capital, with the Order's insignia commonly seen on public buildings and on the chests of aristocracy. Paul's love for the Catholic order is seen as one reason for the putsch against his rule.

The Engineers' Bridge

looking the parade ground and the changing of the guard, shouts strict ceremony. Since Paul I feared an assassination attempt and did not want to stay in the Winter Palace, he gave orders that his new residence should be totally inaccessible to intruders. When it was built, the castle was surrounded by a moat. Drawbridges were lowered down over the canals from the man-made island, guarded by cannons. There was even a secret underground passage which lead to the barracks on the Field of Mars (*see page 59*).

None of these careful precautions, however, managed to save Paul I. Forty days after he had moved into the castle (1801) he was – with the approval of his son, the future Tsar Alexander I – strangled in his bedroom by officers of his personal guard.

Afterwards, members of the imperial family began to avoid the castle. In 1822 it became the address of Russia's first Military Engineering School, which had been started by Peter I in 1712. Field Marshal Kutuzov later attended the school; in 1838 the 16-year-old Dostoyevsky was also sent here. It was while studying in the gloomy Mikhailovsky Castle that he first started to write.

When the adjoining land was redeveloped in 1958, this opened up a magnificent view of the south front of the palace, where a bronze statue of Peter I was erected in 1800. The model for the statue was prepared in 1715 (during Peter I's own lifetime) by Bartolomeo Carlo Rastrelli, the father of the famous architect. The pedestal is adorned with two bas-reliefs: *The Battle of Poltava* and *The Battle of Gangut*, as well as an allegorical composition of trophies.

MAPLE ALLEY

The lane known as Maple Alley (Klenovaya Alleya) runs down what was Paul's parade ground in the 1820s. A little further south is the building which formerly housed the Mikhailovsky Riding School, built between 1788–1801 and renovated by Brenna and Rossi in 1824.

5: The East End

From Nevsky Prospekt, east of the Anichkov Bridge *(see page 55)*, **Liteyny Prospekt**, one of the city's main arteries, leads out to the north. It is named after the foundry (Liteyny Dvor), established in 1711 not far from the Neva Embankment. During Peter I's reign cannons were cast there. The continuation of the Prospekt forms the Liteyny Bridge over the Neva.

Map on page 67

Below: a cosmonaut mural and (bottom) Lenin at Finland Station

LENIN'S STATUE

On the north bank, east of the bridge, is Lenin Square (Ploshchad Lenina) and **Finland Station** ❺ (Finlyandsky Vokzal), a modern concrete structure erected after World War II. In the station courtyard stands a gigantic bronze statue to Lenin designed in 1926 by Yevseyev, Schuko and Gelfreikh. It commemorates a landmark historical event: on the night of 3 April 1917 Lenin returned from exile abroad, having learned about Nicholas II's renunciation of the throne and the fall of the monarchy. From the turret of an armoured car bearing the inscription *Enemy of Capital* he made his famous speech to tens of thousands of workers and soldiers who had flocked to see him.

To the west of Liteyny Prospekt, the **Naberezhnaya Kutuzova** (Kutuzov Embankment)

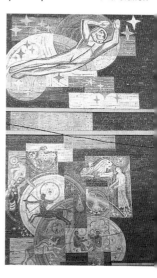

stretches along the south bank of the Neva. It was named after the field commander who also owned a house here (No 3). In 1812 he led the Russian troops to take up arms against Napoleon.

Below: the Tauride Flower Exhibition Hall Bottom: silver birch in the Tauride gardens

SHPALERNAYA ULITSA

Running parallel to Naberezhnaya Kutuzova is **Shpalernaya Ulitsa**. There are many houses here that are of historical significance. In Gagarinskaya Ulitsa, which crosses Shpalernaya Ulitsa, is Countess Yuryevskaya's former palace (No 3). She was the wife of Alexander II in a morganatic marriage. At No 18 is the Mayakovsky Club, St Petersburg's branch of the Writers' Association.

Farther east, Shpalernaya Ulitsa is bordered on the right-hand side by a relatively long line of columns and statues belonging to the former Barracks of the Imperial Guard (end of the 18th century), built in Classical style. On the ground floor the frontage is dominated by a powerful eight-columned Doric portico. Statues of the Ancient Roman god of war, Mars, and the goddess of war, Bellona, stand beside the portico.

TAURIDE PALACE

On the same side of the street, a bit farther on at Shpalernaya Ulitsa 47, is the ★ **Tauride Palace** ㉟

(Tavrichesky Dvorets). It was built on the orders of Catherine II between 1783–9 for her favourite, Gregory Potemkin, and designed by Ivan Starov. Potemkin's conquest of the Crimean peninsula (formerly called Tauris) earned him the title of Count of Tauride. Apparently, before the empress travelled into the deserted area of the Crimea, Potemkin had villages set up like scenery along the route in order to make it look like the area was flourishing.

The reserved, strictly classical lines of the palace's facade, with its use of ancient architectural motifs, compliments its bland interior. When it was built, the palace was one of the largest in Europe (65,700sq m/707,200sq ft). It exerted a considerable influence on Russian architecture over the years and served as a model for many imitations.

Behind the palace a wonderful landscape park was laid out by Volkov, with ponds, canals, islands, grottos, an orangery and wooden pavilions in which lavish parties were held. Only part of the gardens remain today.

After Catherine II's death, her son Paul succeeded to the throne. He hated both his mother and her lover, Potemkin, so ordered the palace to be converted into a barracks and the 36-columned Catherine Ballroom to be used as horse stables.

However, Paul did not reign for very long. His successor, Alexander I, ordered the palace to be restored to its original condition; the palace has remained – since its renovation – unchanged to the present day.

From 1906–17 the imperial parliament sat here. In February 1917 the Petrograd Soviet of Workers and Soldiers' Deputies worked in the left wing of the palace, while the Provisional Committee of Parliament, later to become the Provisional Government, worked in the right wing. After his return from 10 years of exile, it was in this palace that Lenin presented his April thesis, in which he

Talking shop

Today, the Tauride Palace houses the Commonwealth of Independent States' Inter-Parliamentary Assembly. Despite the impressive name, this gathering of the legislatures of the former Soviet republics has little concrete power and authority, and is more akin to a social club that brings powerful lawmakers to the city for conferences and meetings.

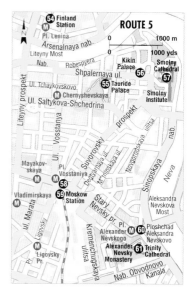

Map on page 67

*Below: the Kikin Palace
Bottom: looking out from the
Smolny at the modern city*

sketched out the transition from a bourgeois society to a socialist one through revolution.

KIKIN PALACE

On the other side of the street, set back from the pavement, is one of the oldest houses in St Petersburg, the **Kikin Palace ㊱** (Kikiny Palati), built in 1714. Its owners were executed because of their involvement in the conspiracy against Peter the Great. The building used to house the collection from the Kunstkamera. Later it was moved to a building on the Vasilievsky Island, specially erected for the purpose *(see page 30)*.

SMOLNY COMPLEX

Shpalernaya Ulitsa ends at Ploshchad Rastrelli, on the east side of which is the **Smolny**, one of the most significant historical monuments of St Petersburg. A number of buildings belong to the group, not all dating from the same period. The oldest complex, the Smolny Institute and the small collegiate Church of the Resurrection, are located on land that used to belong to a tar house (Smolny Dvor), where tar was boiled for Peter the Great's shipyards.

The Empress Elisabeth, daughter of Peter the Great, had a superb park laid out here. Between

1744 and 1760, Bartolomeo Francesco Rastrelli, the master of Russian baroque, erected a convent for the empress, in which she planned to retire eventually. However, her wish was never fulfilled, since she died in 1761. Catherine the Great, who had little sympathy for Elisabeth, soon dismissed Rastrelli from her service.

The crowning glory of Rastrelli's convent consists of the five-towered, opulent ★★★ **Smolny Cathedral ⑰** (Smolny Sobor), built between 1748–64. It was Rastrelli's genius to combine baroque details, such as the highly decorative facade – its sculptured embellishments, columns and richly ornamented trimmings on the windows – with the forest of towers and onion domes typical of an old Russian monastery. The interior of the cathedral, not completed until 1835 by the neo-classical architect Vasiliy Stasov, reflects the austere spirit of classicism, and contrasts dramatically with the luxuriant exterior. Rastrelli arranged nun's cells in a square formation around the cathedral, creating a harmonious ensemble.

Exhibitions and concerts of church music are now held in the cathedral. If you are feeling energetic, you can climb the bell tower for spectacular views of the city.

> **Collegiate church**
> A concert and exhibition hall has been opened in the collegiate church. In the evening concerts include old Russian church instrumental and choral music. Art exhibitions, where the pictures are sold, are also held here. Visitors can enjoy a wonderful panorama of the city from the 63m (206ft) Zvonitsa (belltower).

Smolny Cathedral

SMOLNY INSTITUTE

To the left of the convent, Velten erected the entire ensemble of buildings belonging to the Alexander Institute; a school for the daughters of bourgeois families. To the right of the convent, at Ploshchad Proletarskoy Diktatury 4, is the largest section of the Smolny buildings, the ★ **Smolny Institute**. Intended for the education of girls of aristocratic birth, the institute was built by Quarenghi between 1806 and 1808, and is considered by many to be his masterpiece. Under Soviet rule the courtyard at the back was changed into a flower garden with fountains.

In August 1917 the Smolny had fame thrust upon it when it became the seat of St Petersburg's Soviets, the centre of revolutionary events, and the headquarters of the Bolshevik Central

Map on page 67

History men

City Hall, the seat of the governor, known by locals simply as Smolny, still retains its communist-era statues of Lenin, as well as busts of Marx and Engels. Authorities defend such a decision saying this is part of our history, why should we take it away. The liberal opposition, however, says it makes no sense to publicly honour those who brought suffering, misery, and dictatorship to the country.

Committee. During the night of 25 October, Lenin came here from his last hiding place and took over command of the revolt. That same day he wrote the call: 'To the citizens of Russia', in which he let them know of the dismissal of the Provisional Government and the transfer of power to the revolutionary military committee.

On the same night, the second all-Russian Soviet Congress, meeting in Smolny, passed the two decrees brought in by Lenin concerning Soviet power: the decree concerning peace, which was to introduce peace negotiations with all warring countries, and the decree concerning the dispossession of all large landowners. At the same time the first Soviet Government was formed.

Lenin lived in the Smolny for 124 days before moving his government to Moscow on 10 March 1918. He lived with his wife in two rooms on the first floor. Today, St Petersburg's governor has his offices in the building.

In the avenue leading to the entrance of the Smolny Institute, the busts of Marx and Engels have faced each other since 1932. In front of the entrance itself stands the Lenin memorial, unveiled by Koslov in 1927. Two symmetrical pavilions serve as the entrance to the park, bearing the inscriptions: 'Workers of all countries unite!' and 'The First Soviet of the Proletarian Dictatorship'.

The Smolny Institute

PLOSHCHAD VOSSTANIYA

From the Smolny, the Suvorov Prospekt leads south to **Ploshchad Vosstaniya** ❺❽ (Uprising Square). This square is mainly of historical interest, due to its connection with one of the most decisive events of the Revolution. On 27 February 1917 the Cossacks in Pavlovsky's Guard's Regiment refused to shoot at the unarmed demonstrators who were crossing the square. The Petrograd guard joined together with the workers.

The Alexander Nevsky Monastery and gardens

Until 1917 there was an equestrian statue of Alexander III in this square, whose very solid presence earned it the nickname of 'scarecrow'. After the October Revolution it was transferred to the Russian Museum (there is a small copy in the Alexander Nevsky monastery). In 1985 a stele was placed in the centre of the square in honour of the 'Hero City' of what was then Leningrad, and Alexander III is now in front of the Marble Palace.

The Znamenskaya Church (Znamenskaya Tserkov) which lent the square its original name, was pulled down to make way for the metro station, which opened in 1955. Over the station, rendered outside in granite and inside with red marble, is a large dome. The station is decorated with illustrations portraying the major episodes from the 1917 Revolution.

The **Moscow Railway Station** ❺❾, one of St Petersburg's five train stations, has been in existence since the Moscow–St Petersburg line was opened with great pomp and ceremony on 1 November 1851.

ALEXANDER NEVSKY SQUARE

Alexander Nevsky Square ❻⓿ (Ploshchad Aleksandra Nevskovo) marks the end of the Nevsky Prospekt. It was just a bit farther along the Neva, near the spot where the Izhora flows into the river, that in 1240 Alexander Yaroslavovitch, Count of Novgorod – since then called Nevsky – won his victory over the Swedes, who were commanded by Birger Jarl. In 1938, Sergei Eisenstein used the name of Alexander Nevsky, the man

Russians regard as both a national saint and hero, as the title of his first talking film.

NEVSKY MONASTERY AND CATHEDRAL

As another memorial to Alexander Nevsky, Peter I commissioned the ★★**Alexander Nevsky Monastery** in 1710, which later received the title of *Lavra* (Laura), acquiring certain privileges held by only three other monasteries in Old Russia: the Kiev Monastery of the Caves, the St Sergius Trinity Monastery in Sergiyev Posad and the Potschayevsk Monastery in Volhynien. They were all the seat of an archbishop and all ran a seminary.

In 1724 the relics of Alexander Nevsky were transferred from Vladimir to the monastery. Just behind the monastery's main entrance, left of the main portal, is an 18th-century graveyard, the ★★**Lazarus Cemetery**, also known as the Necropolis. This is the city's oldest cemetery, in which some of Russia's leading cultural figures lie buried *(see panel)*.

The centre of the monastery is the ★★**Trinity Cathedral** ⑥ (Troitsky Sobor), designed by Starov using earlier examples of Russian Classicism as a model and built between 1776–90. It is a tall building with a powerful dome, pushed together, so to speak, by its two belltowers.

The main entrance of the cathedral is decorated with a six-columned portico, embellished by a sculptured gable. Corinthian elements were used in the interior design. Brilliantly executed is the cathedral's iconostasis, for which Italian and Russian marble were used. Also outstanding is the gilded Tsar's Door.

Located in the grounds of the Alexander Nevsky Monastery is the **Church of the Dormition** (Khram Uspenspeniyo Bogoroditsy; 1722, by Domenico Trezzini) containing the **Museum of City Sculpture** (Muzei Skulpturi; open 9.30am– 6pm; closed Thur), as well as the tomb of Suvorov, the great army general.

The best way to get to the monastery is to take the underground to Alexander Nevsky Square (Ploshchad Aleksandra Nevskovo).

Final resting place

The Necropolis of the Alexander Nevsky Lavra is the final resting place of such great figures of Russian culture as Feodor Dostoyevsky, Petr Tchaikovsky, Modest Mussorgsky, and fable writer Ivan Krylov. Besides these famous people, many of the graves are exquisite pieces of sculpture, and are included as part of the collection of the City Museum of Sculpture.

Rimsky-Korsakov's grave

6: The West End

Along the Neva Embankment, west of Decembrists' Square, stretches the Angliskaya (English) Embankment, so called because this was the centre of the British community. Most of the houses on the embankment date from the end of the 18th century.

House No 4 is where the Decembrist, Truhetovsky, lived. The first and second floor of the facade are decorated with 10 Ionic columns. Inside, the sparseness of the vestibule contrasts with the regal stone staircase which leads to the reading room. The **Vorontsov-Dashkov Mansion** (No 10), built in 1738 and renovated in 1770, is a good example of how the facade of a rich villa was designed during the period of early Russian Classicism.

HISTORY MUSEUM

Near the Leytenanta Shmidta Bridge (which was originally the Nikolayevsky Bridge) is the imposing ★ **Museum of the History of St Petersburg**  (Muzey Istorii St Petersburga; open Thur–Tues 11am–5pm; closed Wed), with its massive 12-columned portico and sculptured frieze. The palace originally belonged to Nikolai, the son of Field Marshal Rumyantsev, who

Map on page 74

Star Attraction
● Alexander Nevsky Monastery

Below: interior and (bottom) facade of the History Museum

Map below

Rich past
The St Petersburg History Museum is off the beaten track and not often visited by most tourists, but it merits a visit. The city's history, from its founding in 1703 by Peter the Great, throughout the tsarist, Soviet and World War II periods, are well covered. In 2003, the city marked its 300th anniversary with great fanfare – with many cultural events, as well as a reconstruction of the historical centre.

arranged for the house to be turned into a public museum after his death (1826). The museum contained Rumyantsev's collected works of art, his library, Old Russian and Slavonic handwriting, as well as coin collections and medals. Since 1862 the bulk of the collection has been divided between various museums and institutes (the library, for example, is now in Moscow's National Library). However, there are still some unique exhibits left: hand-drawn city plans and the original sketches of famous Russian architects, whose creations are visible in finished form throughout St Petersburg.

Section 1
The February and October revolutions of 1917: the first years after the October Revolution; Lenin's companions; documentary films; Gorky, Mayakovsky; artists and intellectuals who contributed in one way or another to the establishment of Soviet power.

Section 2
Between the two world wars: the gradual expansion of the city; models, plans, photographs.

Section 3
World War II: the siege and front of the then Leningrad. This section is extremely well-equipped and presents the facts in a fair and unbiased fashion.

Section 4
After World War II: business life. Various branches of business in the city, of which shipbuilding, the clothing industry and the production of precision instruments are the most important.

ENGLISH EMBANKMENT

On the embankment in front of the museum is an obelisk, reminding visitors that it was here that the *Aurora* was anchored *(see page 23)*, the ship whose

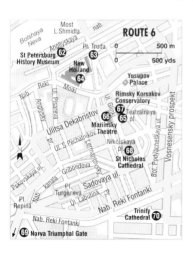

forward cannon fired the historic blank shot that signalled the storming of the Winter Palace.

Another imposing building on the English Embankment (Angliiskaya Naberezhnaya) is the former English Church (No 56), in front of which are three statues. The room once used for prayer, which takes up the entire first floor, is decorated with Corinthian columns.

PLOSHCHAD TRUDA

South of the Leytenanta Shmidta Bridge is **Ploshchad Truda ⓷**. One of the oldest buildings in the square is the **Labour Palace** (Dvorets Truda), formerly belonging to Grand Duke Nicholai Nikolayevitch, and now home to St Petersburg's local trade union committee.

The palace was erected for Nicholas I's son between 1853 and 1861 and designed by Stakenschneider. The wealth of fine decorative embellishments make it an excellent example of 19th-century Russian architecture.

NEW HOLLAND

The triangular-shaped island near the square, formed by the Moika, Kryukov and Admiralteysky Canal, is called ★ **New Holland ⓸** (Novaya Gollandiya). It was here that the wood

Below: the English Embankment
Bottom: New Holland Arch

Map on page 74

Beautiful square

Theatre Square makes up one of the most beautiful architectural ensembles in the city, and includes the Mariinsky Opera and Ballet Theatre and Rimsky-Korsakov Conservatory, while just a little way down the street one can see the impressive golden domes of St Nicholas Cathedral. The old houses around and near the square are considered to be very fashionable and are home to many of the Mariinsky's leading performers.

Mariinsky Theatre iron work

to be used in Peter the Great's shipyards was stacked. The Admiralty Yard and Galley Yard were linked by Galernaya Ulitsa (Galley Street), and by a few canals which, together with the Moika, formed a small island that served as a storage area. The old wooden sheds were soon replaced by brick buildings, and a beautiful granite arch was erected by Vallin de la Mothe. During World War I there was a military radio station here. On 9 November 1917 this station transmitted Lenin's appeal for a cease-fire to all Russian soldiers and sailors on the front.

South of Ploshchad Truda, behind the bridge crossing the Moika, is Ulitsa Glinki. Not far from here, at 8 Pereulok Pirogova, the composer Glinka once lived. Here he composed his famous operas *Ivan Susanin (A Life for the Tsar)* and *Ruslan and Ludmilla*.

THEATRE SQUARE

Ulitsa Glinki runs into the expansive ★★ **Teatralnaya Ploshchad** ❺ (Theatre Square). This is one of the cultural centres of St Petersburg, the city whose people show more appreciation for the theatre than anywhere else in Russia. Established in 1860, the ★★ **Mariinsky Theatre for Opera and Ballet** ❻ has seen such dancers as Anna Pavlova, Vasily Nijinsky and Galina Ulanova, as well as celebrated Russian composers including Katachurian and Prokofiev. The theatre is also the home of the Kirov Ballet Corps which has earned top international acclaim over the years and has retained its Soviet-era name.

During the blockade the theatre was bombarded on numerous occasions. By 1944 renovation work was complete and the doors were reopened with a performance of Glinka's opera *Ivan Susanin (A Life for the Tsar)*.

Opposite the Mariinsky is the late 19th-century **Rimsky Korsakov Conservatory** ❼, Russia's first university of music, designed by Nikol. Its students have included Tchaikovsky, Glazunov and Shostakovich. In front of the building are statues of Glinka and Rimsky-Korsakov.

ST NICHOLAS

South of Teatralnaya Ploshchad, located in Nikol-skaya Ploshchad (St Nicholas Square) is the two-storey ★★ **St Nicholas Cathedral** ❻❽ (Nikolsky Morskoy Sobor). Sometimes called the Sailor's Cathedral, it was designed in the mid-1700s by Chevakinsky, one of Rastrelli's pupils, in Russian baroque style with five domes. A magnificent row of columns, almost Classical in form, adorns the wall of the iconostasis. It is with good reason that these columns are held up as an example of Russian decorative art during that period. The ★★ iconostasis is carved in baroque style, gilded and painted. The cathedral's four-storey belltower stands in splendid isolation by the river.

South of Nikolskaya Ploshchad, Sadovaya Ulitsa runs round the centre of town in a semi-circle, ending at **Ploshchad Repina** (Repin Square), named after the famous Russian realist painter who lived in house No 11 at the end of the 19th century. Repin painted many pictures in this house, including *The Zaporozhian Cossacks write a letter to the Turkish Sultan*.

NARVA SQUARE

About 2km (1 mile) south of Repin Square near the Obvodny Canal lies Narva Square (Narvskaya Ploshchad), scene of the first fatal clashes on

Star Attractions
● Theatre Square
● St Nicholas Cathedral

Below: spire of St Nicholas Cathedral and (bottom) its imposing facade

Map on page 74

Below: the domes of Trinity Cathedral Bottom: Vitebsk Station

'Bloody Sunday' (9 January 1905), when imperial troops opened fire on hundreds of peaceful demonstrators.

In the middle of the square is the **Narva Triumphal Gate** ⓹ (Narvskaya Triumfalnaya Vorota), erected in 1814 to commemorate the victory of the Russian army over Napoleon. The original arch was a wooden structure, hastily put together by Quarenghi, but this was later replaced by Stasov's brick version (1834), duly adorned with statues of great Russian commanders and a statue of Victory riding her six-horsed chariot.

From Narva Square, Ulitsa Pereskopskaya heads northwest to **Catherine Park**, originally laid out by Peter the Great for his second wife, Catherine I. (The palace that once stood here burnt to the ground in 1924.)

The metro station **Kirovsky Zavod** (Kirov Works) is layered with Caucasus marble. The station is dedicated to the workers of the former Putilov Works, the first raiding party of the revolution. The factory also played an important role during the blockade of the city from 1941 to 1944. Production continued at the works, despite the constant bombing all around.

TRINITY CATHEDRAL

To the south of the Fontanka Embankment on Ismailovsky Prospekt is the huge ★ **Trinity Cathedral** ⓻ (Troitsky Sobor), a local landmark with its five dark blue domes. Designed by Stasov between 1827–35, the cathedral is a fine example of Russian neoclassicism. It was here that, according to legend, Peter the Great married a young Livonian washerwoman named Katinka, better known as Empress Catherine I.

Just east of Trinity Cathedral, **Vitebsk Station** was Russia's first train terminal when it opened in 1837. The existing building, dating from 1904, is an exuberant Art Nouveau construction with stained-glass windows and elaborately tiled halls. Also of architectural interest is the **Warsaw Station** on the Obvodny Canal, built at the end of the 19th century.

7: The Islands

This route passes through a fairly large area. Take the car or use the city's public transport facilities.

The islands in the Neva Delta, around which the Great (Bolshaya), Small (Malaya) and Middle (Srednaya) Nevka Rivers flow, are known as Kamenny Ostrov (Stone Island), Yelaginsky Ostrov (Yelagin Island) and Krestovsky Ostrov (Krestovsky Island) or simply the Ostrova (Islands) for short. They once belonged to the nobility. On this land – bequeathed as ancestral estates by Peter the Great to his successors – great architects and landscape gardeners conjured up the country homes of the aristocracy.

The **Islands** were always a favourite place of relaxation for the people of St Petersburg, and after the Revolution they became a fashionable location in which to have a *dacha* (country house). A walk around the islands is an unforgettable experience at any time of year. There are a number of cafés, and lining the avenues are the palaces which used to belong to the nobility and are now used as sanatoriums and rest homes.

Map on pages 80–1

Overdevelopment
St Petersburg was built in the delta of the Neva River, and while much landfill has been done in the past three centuries, there are still many islands on the side of the river opposite the Hermitage. Most of these were home to country estates in tsarist times and are now park areas popular with locals. But local real estate developers have cast a greedy eye on this prime real estate near the city centre and are slowly chipping away at zoning laws restricting construction.

KRESTOVSKY ISLAND

Even before World War II, **Krestovsky Island** had developed into the city's sports centre. The

Reflections at Yelaginsky Ostrov

Map below

Dinamo and Iskra stadiums were opened, followed in 1950 by the **Kirov Stadium ⓲**. Sited on a man-made hill in the sea, it seats 100,000 and is the largest stadium in the country after the Lenin Stadium in Moscow. The Ring Terrace provides a superb view across the Gulf of Finland.

From the stadium, Morskoy Prospekt, one of St Petersburg's most beautiful streets, runs east. The western half of the island, where the Kirov Stadium is located, is occupied by the **Primorsky (Seaside) Park of Victory ⓱**.

The Kirov Stadium

After World War II the population of St Petersburg answered an appeal to help lay the new park, and thousands of citizens joined forces one October Sunday in 1945. A total of 45,000 trees were planted. Today, the park covers a total area of 180 hectares (445 acres).

YELAGIN ISLAND

A bridge across the Middle Nevka links Krestovsky Island with **Yelagin Island**. Alexander I acquired the island in 1817 and made a gift of it to his mother, Empress Maria Fyodorovna. Architect Carlo Rossi and landscape gardener Joseph Busch were commissioned to remodel the island. The result was a large park with a series of man-made lakes and the magnificent, Classical **Yelagin Palace ⓳** (Yelaginsky Dvorets). Its interior, also designed by Rossi, was largely destroyed by fire during World War II, but the

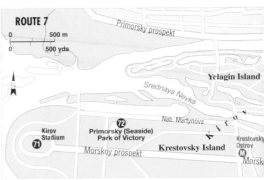

ROUTE 7

0   500 m
0   500 yds

Primorsky prospekt

Yelagin Island

Srednaya Nevka

Nab. Martynova

Kirov Stadium ⓱

⓲ Primorsky (Seaside) Park of Victory

Krestovsky Island

Morskoy prospekt

Krestovsky Ostrov

Ⓜ Morsk

palace was restored a decade later using the old plans. Rossi's other creations on the palace estate are also worth seeing. They include the Orangery, the kitchen wing and stables, the granite harbour and its pavilion as well as the music pavilion.

Until October 1917 Yelagin Island was the summer residence of the tsars, and the park – particularly the western tip – a place of diversion for St Petersburg's aristocracy. Magnificent parties were organised here. It was not until after the Revolution that the park was opened to the general public. In 1932 its name was changed to the Kirov Park of Culture and Relaxation. The island is planted with splendid trees and dotted with small pavilions. Facilities include a summer theatre, a vaudeville theatre, restaurants, sports facilities, beaches and swimming pools. At the western point of the island, the so-called spit or **Strelka**, there is a ** terrace overlooking the Gulf of Finland. The views are superb.

STONE ISLAND

To the east of Yelagin Island is **Stone Island** (Kamenny Ostrov), until recently known as Worker's Island. From the mid-18th century it belonged to Chancellor Betushev-Rumin, who had ponds and canals dug and the embankment fortified with granite slabs. Orangeries and hunting lodges were built here and bridges put over the canals.

Star Attraction
● **view from the terrace at the Strelka**

Boating off Yelagin Island

Map on pages 80–1

Below: the Church of the Birth of John the Baptist
Bottom: cemetery memorial

During the civil war the first rest homes and sanatoriums were opened for workers in what had been the country estates of court aristocrats. These homes acted as a model for Lenin's 1920 decree ordering the creation of spa and rest homes of the same type throughout the country.

Of particular interest on the island is the ★ **Kamennoostrovsky Palace** ❼ (Kamennoostrovsky Dvorets), built by Velten for Paul I between 1776–81. The clear and simple lines of its exterior and interior design make the building an interesting example of Russian Classicism.

The well-preserved **Church of the Birth of John the Baptist** ❼ (Tserkov Roshdestva Ioanna Predtechi) on the Kamennoostrovsky Prospekt was built by Velten between 1776 and 1778. Its pointed tower and lancet windows lend the building a distinctly Gothic appearance.

APOTHECARY ISLAND

As already mentioned, between the south embankment of the Small Nevka and the Karpovka River stretches **Apothecary Island** (Aptekarsky Ostrov), which is dissected from north to south by the Kamennoostrovsky Prospekt. To the east of the Prospekt, near the embankment of the Bolshaya Nevka, is the **Television Tower** ❼ built between 1960 and 1963. It is 316m (1,037ft) high.

Covering an area of 16 hectares (40 acres) at the south-east end of the island is the **Botanical Gardens** ❼ (Botanichesky Sad; open Wed, Sat and Sun 11am–5pm). The garden was first established in 1714 when Peter I planted an apothecary garden with all known medicinal herbs. It was this garden that gave the island its name.

Located in the northern section of the garden is the **Russian Botanical Museum**, which looks after one of the largest herbariums in the world, with over 100,000 exhibits.

About 3km (1½ miles) to the northeast of Finland Station is the famous ★ **Piskarev Cemetery** (Piskaryovskoye Kladbische), where over 500,000 victims of the Nazi Siege or *Blokada* lie buried in mass graves.

8: Moskovsky Prospekt

Map
on page
84

This route cannot be described as scenic per se,
since the six-lane **Moskovsky Prospekt** (Moscow
Prospect) offers nothing really worth seeing apart
from buildings dating from the Stalinist era. However, anybody driving to or from the airport,
Pushkin or Pavlovsk, has to use this road, hence
its most important buildings deserve a mention.

The Prospekt begins at Sennaya Ploshchad in
the city centre, crosses the Fontanka and Obvodny
Canals, continues south in a dead-straight line past
the Moskovsky Triumphal Arch and eventually
becomes Highway 10, the main road to Moscow
and Novgorod. It was on this road that Radischev
left St Petersburg on the trip he describes in his
book: *A Trip from St Petersburg to Moscow*.

INSTITUTE OF TECHNOLOGY

Founded in 1828, the **Institute of Technology** 🕖
(Technologichesky Instituta) lies just south of the
Fontanka Canal, at the intersection with Zagorodny
Prospekt. It is considered one of the leading uni-
versities of the city. On the opposite side of Mos-
kovsky Prospekt at No 19в is the Scientific
Research Institute for Meteorology (Mendeleyev
Institute). A monument to the great Russian scholar,
and what is purported to be the most precise clock

Mendeleyev
D.I. Mendeleyev (1834–
1907) was one of Russia's
greatest scientists. His most important
contribution to scientific knowledge
was the discovery of chemical peri-
odicity; the arrangement of elements
(across a 'periodic table') according
to their behaviour and the number
and distribution of their electrons.

The Technology Institute

in the world, stand in the courtyard. Decorating one wall is an enormous mosaic showing, in picture form, the periodic law of atomic weights formulated by Mendeleyev. Nearby, at No 28, is the vestibule of the Institute of Technology, decorated with 28 bronze medallions of Russian scholars, including Lomonosov, Mendeleyev and Pavlov.

PLEKHANOV HOUSE

On the corner of Moskovsky Prospekt/ Krasnoarmeyskaya Ulitsa is **Plekhanov House** ⑦ (Dom Plekhanova), built in 1800. The Free Economy Company used to have its headquarters in what was once the home of George Plekhanov (1856–1918), the 'father of Russian Marxism'. Lenin frequently visited the house, which was used as a secret meeting place. In 1905 St Petersburg's first soviets held meetings here. In a side wing of the building are Plekhanov's files and library, bequeathed by his widow to the history and science department of the Russian National Library, of which this house is now a subsidiary.

Another example of fine architecture is house No 65 at the other side of the Obvodny Canal, the entrance to the former slaughterhouse (1825, by Charlemagne).

On the left in house No 98 is the **Soyuz Pushnina** (The House of Fur); here, international fur auctions and exhibitions are held each January, July and October. Behind this building is the **Convent of the Virgin** (Novodevichy Monastyr), where the poets Tutchev and Nekrasov are buried.

TRIUMPHAL ARCH

Commemorating the victory of the Russian army over Turkey (1828) is the **Moscow Triumphal Arch** ⑧ (Moskovskaya Vorota). Twelve cast-iron Doric columns form the imposing arch, designed by Stasov and erected between 1833 and 1838. The height of the gate measures 25m (82ft). In the first half of the 19th century the arch was also the gate to the city. Next to it stood a guard house, where travellers' papers were checked.

VICTORY PARK

The main entrance to ★ **Moskovsky Park Pobedy**
⓫ (Moscow Victory Park) is located opposite the
nine-storey Rossiya Hotel. This park was laid out
by volunteer labour in 1945, and flanking Heroes'
Avenue, which runs straight through it, are bronze
busts of various noble citizens who fought for
St Petersburg. The fountain at the end shoots an
11m (36ft) jet of water. The 70-hectare (173-acre)
park, with its man-made ponds and islands, is a
favourite leisure spot for the local populace.

At the south end of the park, situated in Ulitsa
Gastello, is the unique **Chesma Palace** (closed to
the public). Built by Velten, this is where Catherine II would stay on her way to Tsarskoe Selo.
Equally alluring is the red-and-white striped
Chesma Church which stands behind the palace,
built by the same architect.

To the east, at No 8 Gagarina Ulitsa (Gagarin
Street), stands the modern, circular building of
the largest sports and leisure complex in the city,
the SKK (Sportivo Kontsertny Kompleks).

Moskovsky Prospekt ends at **Victory Square**
⓬ (Ploshchad Pobedy), with a monument hon-
ouring the citizens who defended the city. Issu-
ing from the central round tower are the roads
to Novgorod and Moscow, the road to Pulkovo,
Pushkin, Pavlovsk and the airport and the road
to Petrodvorets.

Old observatory
From Victory Square, in the
distance it is possible to see
Pulkovo Hill, crowned by the oldest
observatory in Russia, the Pulkovo
Observatory (the former Nicholas
Observatory), built in 1839. During
the siege, the observatory, including
its optical instruments and library (the
largest on astronomy in the world)
was almost totally destroyed. But the
establishment has since been renovated and expanded.

Below: Victory Park
Bottom: Chesma Church

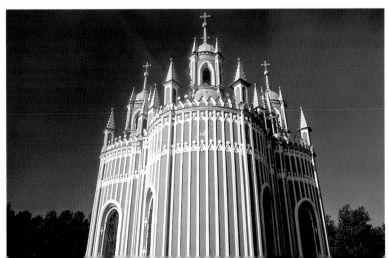

The Hermitage Museum

It is worth going to St Petersburg just to see the treasures housed in the internationally renowned Hermitage Museum in the Winter Palace, 34 Dvortsovaya Naberezhnaya (Palace Embankment; open Tues–Sat 10.30am–6pm, Sun and holidays 10.30am–5pm; closed Mon).

BACKGROUND

The Hermitage Museum occupies several now-connected buildings, the largest of which is the **★★★ Winter Palace**, the former imperial residence *(see page 41)* and part of the museum since 1946. Overlooking Palace Square is the **Small Hermitage**, which Catherine II had built between 1764–75 by the architect Vallin de la Mothe, who was teaching architecture at the Academy of Art at the time. The construction satisfied the empress's desire for a new palace in which to house her art collections; shortly afterwards she united the Small Hermitage with the Winter Palace. The **Second** or **Old Hermitage** was erected on the Neva Embankment between 1771–87 by Velten, also for Catherine's collections.

The **Hermitage Theatre** is separated from the main building by a canal, and may be reached by a bridge reminiscent in shape of those in Venice and Amsterdam. Built by Quarenghi in 1783–7, the theatre is now open for public concerts and performances.

Ten giant granite Atlantes sculpted by Alexander Terebenyev support the portal of the **New Hermitage**, on Millionnaya Ulitsa (Millionaires' Street). Nicholas I had the palace built to the designs of Leo von Klenze between 1839–52 as a museum open to the general public. It was opened with great ceremony in 1852.

At the outbreak of World War II, the museum's treasures were taken to a secure place. The most important objects (1,118,000 in total) were stored in areas beyond the Urals and in Central Asia.

In 1995 a stunning collection of 75 Impressionist and Post-Impressionist paintings taken

Star Attraction
● Winter Palace

👁 **World famous**
The Hermitage ranks among the top four museums of the world, along with London's British Museum, New York's Metropolitan Museum of Art, and Paris's Louvre. It has a collection of almost three million items, though one million are coins, but less than five percent of the collection is on display. The museum recently acquired a new building, the General Staff Building on Palace Square, now under restoration; this project is due to cost $150 million but it will add about 40,000 square metres (430,500 sq ft) of display space.

Opposite: the Jordan Staircase
Below: the Herm of Hermes

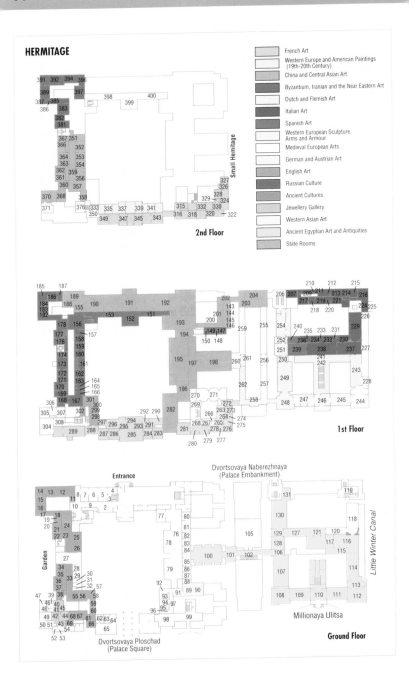

HERMITAGE

	French Art
	Western Europe and American Paintings (19th-20th Century)
	China and Central Asian Art
	Byzantium, Iranian and the Near Eastern Art
	Dutch and Flemish Art
	Italian Art
	Spanish Art
	Western European Sculpture, Arms and Armour
	Medieval European Arts
	German and Austrian Art
	English Art
	Russian Culture
	Ancient Cultures
	Jewellery Gallery
	Western Asian Art
	Ancient Egyptian Art and Antiquities
	State Rooms

2nd Floor

Small Hermitage

1st Floor

Dvortsovaya Naberezhnaya
(Palace Embankment)

Entrance

Garden

Little Winter Canal

Millionaya Ulitsa

Ground Floor

Dvortsovaya Ploschad
(Palace Square)

from Germany during the war and believed lost was put on display. The paintings remain on show, though their future is uncertain since Germany insists on their return.

Map opposite

THE PALACE ROOMS

Before looking at the myriad art works, it is recommended that you first visit the magnificent State rooms of the Winter Palace. These are found on the first floor. After buying an entrance ticket turn left, cross the long columned gallery to arrive at the imposing ★★ **Jordan Staircase**, made of Carrara marble and decorated with sculptures, gold plating and stucco. This architectural pièce de résistance was built by Rastrelli and restored by Stasov after the catastrophic fire of 1837, which devastated the Winter Palace.

Directly in front of you, at the top of the staircase, is an **Antechamber** containing the Empire-style **Rotunda**, a round canopy supported by eight malachite columns. This leads on to the ★ **Nikolaev Hall**, the largest room in the Winter Palace. Now used for temporary exhibitions, this magnificent white-and-gold hall, lit by monumental crystal chandeliers, was previously the scene of official ceremonies and lavish balls.

Pass on into the **Concert Hall**. Here, in addition to the Russian silver pieces from the end of the 17th to the early 20th centuries, is one of the biggest treasures of the museum: ★**Alexander Nevsky's silver sarcophagus**. Empress Elisabeth Petrovna had this richly ornamented tomb made in 1752 out of the imperial coins minted from the first 1,474kg (3,250lbs) of silver mined in Kolyvan, Siberia. The sarchophagus was intended for the remains of St Alexander Nevsky, which are now in the Alexander Nevsky Lavra, and bas-reliefs on the exterior show scenes from the saint's life.

Continue across the Concert Hall to the ★ **Malachite Drawing-Room**, completed in 1839 under the architect Alexander Bryullov. The splendid green of the Ural malachite contrasts impressively with the gold of the chandeliers, capitals and ornate ceiling decoration.

Star Attraction
● Jordan Staircase

Getting in
The ticket desks, situated in the foyer opposite the entrance, are open until an hour before the museum closes. It is much more practical, however, to buy the tickets from your hotel. At least half a day is necessary to visit the Hermitage, and a second trip is recommended to do it justice.

Jordan Staircase detail

Map on page 88

Below: a blue vase from the Golden Salon
Bottom: a mosaic floor in the Pavilion Hall

Situated just off the Malachite Drawing-Room is the former **Small Dining Room** of the Winter Palace, in which members of the Provisional Government were arrested. The room has been preserved exactly as it was on that fateful occasion.

Retrace your steps to the Jordan Staircase via **The Rotunda** and **The Portrait Gallery of the Romanovs**. The Rotunda is a circular room with a coffered dome, which contains an ivory chandelier made on one of the palace's lathes. Also here is a model of a victory column, intended for a St Petersburg square, and the uniform that Peter the Great wore at the Battle of Poltava. In The Portrait Gallery of the Romanovs, a long corridor parallel to the Great Hall, are paintings of the Russian royal family, notably works depicting Elisabeth Petrovna, Catherine II and Paul I.

Off the half-landing at the top of the Jordan Staircase is the **Field Marshal's Hall**, named after the marshals whose portraits decorate the walls. Pass through to the ★★ **Small Throne Room**, designed in 1833 by Auguste Montferrand. The walls are lined with crimson velvet from Lyon and strewn with Romanov eagles. At the back is the semi-circular exedra, home to the throne of Peter the Great; above the throne is Jacopo Amigoni's painting *The Tsar and Minerva* (1732–4).

The next room is the vast **Armorial Hall**, which contains the coats of arms of the different

Russian provinces, as well as a permanent exhibition of Russian costumes. Receptions were once held in this room. Off to the left, via the **1812 War Gallery**, is the ★★ **St George (or Great Throne) Room**. Built by Giacomo Quarenghi, this room is enormous (940 sq m/10,118sq ft). Its parquet flooring, with a bronze motif that mirrors the ceiling decoration, is made from 16 precious woods. The 48 columns made out of white Carrara marble are crowned with bronze capitals. At the back of the room there is the imperial throne with a bas-relief by Francesco del Dero (after designs by Stasov) depicting St George killing the dragon.

In the Small Hermitage, note Andrei Stackenschneider's 19th-century **Pavilion Hall**, a grand room with marble columns, gilded bronze balconies and 28 chandeliers. The Hall houses **The Peacock Clock**, crafted by the English jeweller James Coxe in the 18th century and still ticking.

Star Attractions
- Small Throne Room
- Great Throne Room

Soviet reminders
The Winter Palace's Great Throne Room was restored to its original grandeur in 2000, and Soviet pieces, such as a huge mosaic map of the USSR made of semi-precious stones that hung in the room during Soviet times, have been put in storage.

The Main Sections

The art collections housed in the Hermitage Museum are divided into seven different sections:
- **Western European art and culture**
- **Russian art and culture**
- **Antiquities of the former Soviet Union**
- **Antiquities of the Near and Middle East**
- **Classical antiquities**
- **Art and culture of the Middle and Far East (outside the former Soviet Union)**
- **Coin collection**

The collections of the Hermitage defy comprehension, and it is estimated that it would take eight hours a day for 70 years for someone to see all the exhibits. There are, however, undoubted highlights for any visitor. These include the state rooms already mentioned and the collections described below. Other sections well worth looking at include the ★**Japanese wood carvings**, some exquisite ★**Indian Mughal miniatures** and important ★**Byzantine icons**. In addition,

The Golden Salon

Map
on page
88

the Hermitage contains the world's largest collection of **Sassanid silver dishes**.

THE ALTAI AND SCYTHIAN RELICS

Below: a Scythian sculpture and (bottom) large bronze cauldron

The most important exhibits in the museum are the ★★ **Altai and Scythian relics and artefacts**. The Altai finds from Central Asia and Siberia, dated to the 5th–4th century BC, largely come from excavations of burial mounds. These earth mounds had remained frozen for much of their history and so preserved many of the objects within them in near pristine condition, including pieces made of organic materials such as wood and felt that decay under normal conditions.

Among the prize exhibits are two of **the world's oldest carpets** – both from Southern Siberia – one an appliqué felt representation of a warrior on horseback approaching a female deity, the other a very fine woollen knotted carpet with concentric borders of animals.

Other highlights to look out for include a wooden carving of a **griffon's head** and a wonderful felt **model of a swan**. In the belief system of the ancient people of the Altai, the swan unified the three elements of the universe: ground, water and air.

Perhaps the most striking of the excavated objects, however, is the 3-metre- (10-ft-) high **hearse**. Constructed entirely of wood (all the

pieces are joined by small wooden pegs) it was found in pieces and painstakingly reconstructed by experts from the museum.

The Scythian finds mostly come from burials in the Crimea and along the Dnieper and Don. The most precious items are the Scythian gold artefacts, held in both the Golden Treasures Gallery (*see below*) and the Diamond Gallery. Scythian art draws heavily on animal motifs, and many of the objects in the collection are decorated with representations of deer, leopards and other animals. Notable are the **ram's head bridle** carved out of bone, and the **bronze staff head** in the shape of a stylised bird.

THE GOLDEN TREASURES GALLERY

The stunning ancient jewellery collections may only be visited on a guided tour (tel: 812-3118 446). The pieces held here are priceless and range from exquisite Scythian and Greek items, to Byzantine and Mughal treasures. The Hermitage has one of the finest collections of gold jewellery in the world, stored in a specially designed vault.

Of particular note among the Scythian jewellery are two beautiful pieces: the '**Kelermess panther**' and the '**Kostroma deer**'. Both stem from the Black Sea coast and date from the 7th century BC, and it is thought they were used as the centrepieces of shields.

The influence of the Hellenic world on the Black Sea region grew over the next three centuries and some of the later Scythian pieces have a distinct Greek influence, in particular the **pendant with a depiction of Athena** (4th century BC).

Among the Mughal items on display are a **ring** belonging to Shah Jahan, some beautiful enamel work and a **gem-encrusted pitcher** used to hold rose water. The pieces were donated to the museum in 1741 by Nadir Shah, the Persian ruler who sacked Delhi in 1739.

As well as an extensive collection of **Chinese jewellery** – mostly dating from the 17th and 18th centuries – there are some fascinating examples of **South American gold**.

Star Attraction
● Altai and Scythian relics and artefacts

Non-Western displays
Contrary to popular opinion, the Hermitage Museum not only has a great collection of European art, but also a fine collection of 18th-century Russian artefacts, Russian icons, as well as items relating to the history of the other nations that populate the territory of Russia and the former Soviet Union.

Scythian pendant in the shape of a panther

Map on page 88

FRENCH ART

There are over 50 rooms of French art spanning five centuries in the Hermitage, comprising one of the greatest collections in the museum. The ★★ **collections of Impressionist and Post-Impressionist art** are particularly impressive.

17TH- AND 18TH-CENTURY PAINTING

Below: Conversation by Matisse, 1910
Bottom: the Poussin Room

In painting, French Classicism emerged during the first half of the 17th century, chiefly though the works of **Poussin**. The ★★ **Poussin Room** contains a number of this artist's best canvases, including *Landscape with Polyphemus* (1649). The other important 17th-century artist well represented in the Hermitage is the much-admired landscape painter **Claude Lorraine**.

With the advent of the 18th century there came a change of style exemplified by the great painters of the French Rococo: **Watteau** (look for his *Savoyard with a Marmot*,1716), **Boucher** (see his *Pastoral Scene*, very characteristic of the period) and **Fragonard** (painter of the delightful *Stolen Kiss*), who are all well represented in the collections. At the same time artists such as **Chardin** were producing realist still lifes and genre paintings (his *Still Life with the Attributes of the Arts* (1766) was commissioned by Catherine II).

19TH-CENTURY PAINTING

The end of the 18th century ushered in Romanticism and neoclassicism. The former is represented in the Hermitage by some superb paintings by **Delacroix**, in particular the Orientalist *Arab Saddling his Horse* (1855) and his emotive *Lion Hunt in Morocco* (1854). Paintings by the neoclassical painters **David** and **Ingres** include the former's *Sappho and Phaon* (1809) and the latter's *Count Nikolai Guryev* (1821).

IMPRESSIONISM AND POST-IMPRESSIONISM

The museum's coverage of French Impressionism is wonderful, with paintings from across the period enabling the visitor to see the chronological development of the movement. Among the works by **Monet**, look out for his early *Lady in a Garden*; this was a revelation to his contemporaries owing to its ground-breaking sensitivity to light, tones and reflections. Note also the atmospheric *Pond at Montgeron* (1876–7) and the late picture of *Waterloo Bridge in the Mist* (1903).

Other well-represented exponents of the Movement include **Renoir**, **Pissarro** and **Degas**. Note Renoir's *Portrait of the Actress Jeanne Samary* (1878), Pissarro's virtuoso *Boulevard Montmartre in Paris* (1897) and Degas's stunning pastel of a *Woman Combing Her Hair* (1885).

Some of the most celebrated works of **Matisse**, **Van Gogh**, **Gaughin** and **Cézanne** are also to be found in the Hermitage. They were acquired due to the fine tastes of turn-of-the-20th-century industrialists and art collectors, Sergei Shchukin and Ivan Morozov, who recognized great art in works by Matisse and Cézanne which French critics panned. As a result, the Hermitage now has the largest Matisse collection in the world. Notable paintings include Cézanne's *Still Life with Curtain* (1894–5), Van Gogh's *Women of Arles* (1888), Gaugin's *Woman Holding a Fruit* (1893) and Matisse's *Red Room* (1908) and *The Dance* (1909–10). The Hermitage also has a superb collection of cubist paintings by ★★ **Picasso**, including his *Guitar and Violin* (1913).

Star Attractions
- Impressionist and Post-Impressionist art
- Poussin Room
- Picasso's cubist paintings

Cameos and combs
The Hermitage's collections of painting are not all on a grand scale. For a glimpse of western European painting on a miniature scale head for the Golden Salon. Here there is a ★ **collection of more than 1,000 cameos and combs** by western European masters.

Renoir's Jeanne Samary

Map on page 88

Map on page 88

👁 **German art**
Foremost among the works in the Hermitage's impressive German collection are the works of **Lucas Cranach the Elder**, including *The Virgin and Child under the Apple Tree* (1530) and his *Portrait of a Woman* (1526). Other gems include the *Portrait of a Young Man* by **Ambrosius Holbein** (1518), a *Self Portrait* by **Angelica Kauffman** (1780–5) and *On Board a Sailing Ship* by **Friedrich** (1818–20).

The Italian Art Hall

ITALIAN ART

Spread over 30 rooms, the extensive holdings of Italian painting and sculpture date from the 13th to the 18th century. These works made their way to Russia during tsarist times, when members of the Russian aristocracy, who often visited and even maintained residences in Italy, spared little expense to acquire fine art.

The greatest stars of the Hermitage's Italian collection are two canvases by **Leonardo da Vinci** (1452–1519), *Benois Madonna* and *Madonna Litta* (representing a sixth of his surviving paintings), as well as two masterpieces by ★★**Raphael** (1483–1520), *The Holy Family* and *Madonna Conestabile,* and a mannerist sculpture by **Michelangelo**: *Young Boy Crouching*. However, there is much more to the collections than just these pieces.

PRE-15TH-CENTURY WORKS

Among the pre-Renaissance works, one of the earliest is the Byzantine-influenced *Cross with the Crucified Christ* (*c* 1265) by **Uglino di Tedice**. Also showing the influence of Byzantium, is the slightly later *Madonna of the Annunciation* by **Simone Martini** (1284–1344). The graceful lines of the Madonna's pose were intended to act in counterpoint to the opposing panel of a triptych (which is now in the National Gallery of Art, Washington).

THE RENAISSANCE

With the dawn of the Renaissance (the 'rebirth' of Classical ideals) in the early 15th century, conventions of parallel perspective and classical allusion were adopted in Italian painting. Works from this period include *Madonna and Child with Saints Dominic and Thomas Aquinas* (1430) by **Fra Beato Angelico**, *The Vision of St Augustine*, 1450–60 by **Fra Filippo Lippi** and *The Adoration of the Infant Christ* (1480) by his son, **Filippo Lippi**.

By the beginning of the 16th century Italian art entered the period referred to as the High

Renaissance (*c* 1500–27). This was, above all, characterised by the work of three artists, Raphael, Michelangelo and Leonardo da Vinci, all represented in the Hermitage collections. Apart from masterpieces by these artists (highlighted above), the museum also has works by **Giorgione** (*Judith*), **Corregio** (*Portrait of a Woman*, 1519) and **Cesare da Sesto** (*The Holy Family with St Catherine*, 1515–20).

The great works by **Titian** found in the Hermitage date from slightly later (between 1530 and 1570). Outstanding are his *Danaë*, *Portrait of a Young Woman* (1536) and one of his last paintings, *St Sebastian* (1570).

POST-RENAISSANCE PAINTING

The two Venetian near-contemporaries **Tintoretto** and **Veronese** are both well represented in the Hermitage collections. The former's works include the *Birth of John the Baptist* (1554–5), while of the latter, *The Adoration of the Magi* (1570) and a superb *Pietà* (1576–82), can both be seen. The museum also has some fine works by **Caravaggio**, of which perhaps the best known is *The Lute Player* (1595).

From the 18th century is the wonderful *Maecenas Presenting the Liberal Arts to Augustus* (1745) by **Tiepolo**, and a number of works by **Guardi**.

Star Attraction
● **Raphael paintings**

Below: the Madonna Litta
by Leonardo da Vinci
Bottom: the Lute Player
by Caravaggio

Greek connection
Many fine ancient Greek artefacts came to the Hermitage from the Crimea region, which Russia conquered in the latter part of the 18th century. The Crimea and most of the Black Sea coast were controlled by ancient Greek city-states, and boasted large cities, such as Pantikapae (now Kerch in Ukraine), which was the fourth largest ancient Greek city.

SPANISH ART

One of the best collections of Spanish painting outside Spain itself, the Hermitage works were mostly acquired in the early 19th century, following the Napoleonic Iberian campaigns that spread awareness of Spanish art throughout Europe.

The earliest pieces are from the late-15th century and show the influence of the International Gothic style, then dominant in Spain. The first works by named painters date from the 16th century and include a *Virgin and Child* (1570) by **Morales** and a late work, *St Peter and St Paul* (1587–92), by **El Greco**, who had moved to Spain at the age of 36.

The most impressive part of the collection dates from the 17th century, the so-called 'Golden Age' of Spanish painting. Outstanding among these works are two by **Velázquez**: the early *Luncheon* (1617) and the wonderful *Portrait of Count Olivares* (1640). The Hermitage has a particularly rich collection of paintings by **Murillo**; works on display include the genre painting *Boy with a Dog* (1655–60) and the monumental *Immaculate Conception* (1670) and *Rest on the Flight into Egypt* (1655–70).

Among later Spanish painters, the Hermitage posseses one painting by **Goya**, the *Portrait of Actress Antonia Sarate* (1810–11).

Rembrandt's Danaë

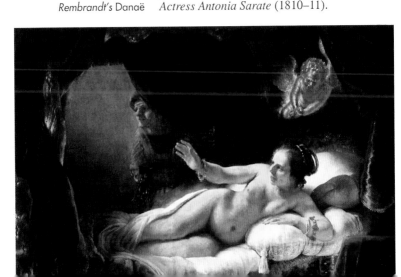

DUTCH AND FLEMISH ART

The Hermitage's Dutch and Flemish works are on a par with the museum's impressive collections of French painting. Their extraordinary range and quality make this one of the most important collections in the world. Of particular note are the three rooms dedicated to ★★ **Van Dyck**, ★★ **Rubens** and ★★ **Rembrandt** respectively.

15TH- AND 16TH-CENTURY PAINTING

Among the earlier works is the diptych by **Robert Campin**, *the Trinity* and *Madonna and Child by the Fireplace* (1430), painted in oils – a new technique at the time. Also outstanding is *St Luke Drawing a Picture of the Virgin* by **van der Weyden** (one of Campin's students).

Also of interest are two paintings by **Pieter Bruegel the Younger**, *The Adoration of the Magi* and *The Sermon of John the Baptist*, both copies of works by his father.

17TH-CENTURY PAINTING

Of particular richness are the works dating from the 17th century. (There are so many that only a selection is on display at any one time.) Of the 22 paintings by Rubens, works to look out for include: *Portrait of a Lady-in-Waiting to the Infanta Isabella* (c 1625), *The Union of Earth and Water* (1618) and *Bacchus* (1638–44); the latter is based on a bust of the Roman Emperor Vitellius.

One of the greatest works in the Hermitage is Van Dyke's *Self Portrait* of 1622–3, as well as his *Portrait of Court Ladies* (c 1638), which was painted in England. The Hermitage also has some truly outstanding paintings by Rembrandt, notably: *Saskia as Flora* (1634), *Danaë* (1636) and *The Return of the Prodigal Son* (1668–9), one of his very last paintings.

Other gems of the collection include the *Mistress and Her Maid* by **de Hooch** (1660), a *Portrait of a Young Man* by **Hals** (1650) and *The Fishmonger's Shop* (1620) by **Snyders**.

Star Attraction
● **paintings by Van Dyck, Rubens and Rembrandt**

Below: Union of Earth and Water *by Rubens*
Bottom: Murillo's Boy with Dog

Map on page 102

Opulent palaces

Not content with having huge and luxurious dwellings within the city, Russia's imperial rulers felt the need to construct ever-more opulent palace complexes in the neighbouring countryside. The effect of these extraordinary displays of wealth amongst the dire poverty experienced by ordinary Russians came home to roost in 1917.

Excursions

St Petersburg's southwest suburb is home to five major imperial residences: Peterhof, Oranienbaum (Lomonosov), the Catherine Palace, Pavlovsk and Gatchina. The last three are still under reconstruction from damage sustained by the Nazis during World War II, but are partly open to the public. Besides the magnificent palace structures, each has beautiful parks and gardens. It is not possible to get a complete picture of St Petersburg without making a visit to at least one of these destinations.

The final excursion highlighted here is to Repino, northeast of St Petersburg, where Ilya Repin, one of Russia's greatest artists, lived.

PETERHOF (PETRODVORETS)

Situated 29km (18 miles) from St Petersburg on the southern shore of the Gulf of Finland, Peterhof is one of the most magnificent country estates of the 18th century. This Russian Versailles was commissioned by Peter I and its centrepiece is the ★★★ **Grand Palace** (open 10am–5pm; closed Mon and last Tues of the month), located between the Upper and Lower Parks. Erected by Jean Baptiste Alexandre Leblond, the palace was completely remodelled in the middle of the 18th century by Bartolomeo Francesco Rastrelli. He added the two side wings and galleries, thus connecting the main building to the castle chapel in the east and the pavilion bearing the coat of arms in the west.

Before World War II the rooms, salons, galleries and wings were an extravagent show of splendour. During the war practically everything was devastated – renovation work has still not been finished, but completed sections include the 270m/886ft facade of the central section (early baroque), the roof, the domes, the cast-iron balcony railings and some of the most important rooms.

Inside the palace, in addition to exhibitions of decorative and applied art, there is also a collection of 368 portraits by Italian painters from the 18th century.

Peterhof fountain detail

SPECTACULAR GARDENS

The terraced, landscaped park (approximately 800 hectares/1,977 acres) descends to the sea; scattered between the 142 waterfalls and fountains are small palaces and pavilions. The ★★**Grand Cascade**, one of the largest fountain ensembles in the world, is particularly spectacular. The best views are from the terrace in front of the Grand Palace. This masterpiece of landscape gardening consists of 37 gilded statues, 150 decorative sculptures, 29 bas-reliefs, two sets of steps leading up to the cascade, 64 fountains and a wonderful grotto. In the middle of a semicircular basin stands a gilded Samson, holding apart the jaws of a lion, out of which spurts a 20m (66ft) fountain. From the cascade a canal leads directly into the open sea. The tsar always used the sea route when he was travelling to Peterhof from St Petersburg.

The Lower Park forms a green backdrop to the Samson basin. The park was laid out in the 18th century and covers an area of 102.5 hectares (253 acres). Over 2,000 jets of water spurt from its 150 fountains. On the eastern side of the park is the Shakhmatnaya Gorka Cascade (1721, by Zemtsov), in front of which stand two powerful fountains – the Roman Fountains (1739 by Blank and Davydov; altered by Rastrelli at the end of the 18th century), which in their original form were reminiscent of the fountains in front of St

Star Attractions
● Grand Palace
● Grand Cascade

Below: Peterhof's exquisite staircase
Bottom: the Grand Cascade

Map below

Peterhof piano and portraits

Peter's Church in Rome. One of the avenues from the Roman Fountains leads to the huge Pyramid Fountain, so-named because its 505 jets of different heights form a pyramid of water.

Also of interest are the Sun Fountains and the series of Shutichi Fountains (from the word *shutka*, meaning joke). The western section of the Lower Park uses the same plan as in the east, although it appears to be different thanks to the innovations of the architect.

ORANIENBAUM (LOMONOSOV)

Just 11 km (7 miles) west of Peterhof, on a hill facing the sea, sits the imposing palace of Peter the Great's favourite, Count Menshikov. The Great Palace of Oranienbaum (open 10.30am–5pm; closed Mon and last Tues of the month) was built in the Russian baroque style between 1710–25, and was far more ambitious in conception than Peterhof. The Chinese Palace was erected in Catherine the Great's reign (built by Rinaldi, 1762–68). Dubbed 'Her Majesty's private *dacha*', it is famous for its exquisite Rococo interiors and fine displays of chinoiserie.

TSARSKOE SELO (PUSHKIN)

The palace at Tsarskoe Selo (25km/16 miles from St Petersburg) was a present from Peter the Great to his wife Catherine I. Between 1719 and 1723, the former country house was transformed into the magnificent ★★★ **Catherine Palace** (Yekaterinsky Dvorets; open 10am–6pm; closed Tues and last Mon of the month). Retained in its original rococo style, it is one of the most richly furnished palaces in the environs of St Petersburg and is without doubt one of Rastrelli's finest creations. It was completely destroyed during World War II and the restoration work is still being completed.

The palace is surrounded by a park with monuments and sculptures by Italian masters. One wing housed the grammar school. Alexander Pushkin attended this school (for the privileged classes) from 1811 to 1817. Today the school has become a subsidiary of the Pushkin Museum. To honour their past pupil, the town of Tsarskoe Selo was renamed Pushkin in the 1930s.

PAVLOVSK

Just 2km (1 mile) southeast of Tsarskoe Selo lies another extraordinary palace and park. In 1777, Catherine II made a gift of the land on the banks of the River Slavyanka to her son, the future Tsar Paul I, in reward for the birth of a grandson who would continue the dynasty. World-famous architect Charles Cameron was commissioned to design both palace and park, and Vincenzo Brenna later replaced him. With the buildings and the park forming a harmonious whole, Pavlovsk was to become one of the most significant monuments to art by the turn of the 19th century.

The centrepiece of the ensemble is the ★★ **Grand Palace** (Bolshoy Dvorets; open 10.30am–5pm; closed Fri, and first Mon of month in winter). Today, there are 45 rooms open in the palace's museum, including the Italian and Greek rooms, the Carpet Cabinet, the War and Peace Room, the Throne Room, the Dining Room and the Portrait Gallery. In the palace there is an exhibition of

Star Attractions
● Catherine Palace
● Grand Palace

Rastrelli
A favoured architect of the early Romanov rulers living in St Petersburg, Bartolomeo Rastrelli (1700–71) was responsible for some of the most imposing edifices in and around the city. Some of his best work can be seen in the design of the Catherine and Winter Palaces.

The Catherine Palace

Map on page 102

Grand designs
The Catherine Palace was in fact named for the wife of Peter the Great, Catherine I, who ruled Russia after his death from 1725 to 1727. Catherine the Great, who is also Catherine II, greatly enlarged the palace during her reign in the last third of the 18th century. The palace is home to the fabled Amber Room, which was stolen and lost during World War II, but was rebuilt by Russian craftsmen and opened anew in May 2003.

Russian interiors from the 18th to 19th century. The 600-hectare (1,483- acre) park is laid out partly in French and partly in English style, dotted with pavilions and romantic ruins. The Visconti Bridge, designed by Voronikhin in 1807, is one of the most famous to cross the Slavyanka.

GATCHINA

In 1765, Catherine II presented Gatchina, located 45km (28 miles) south of St Petersburg, to her lover, Grigory Orlov. He commissioned Rinaldi to build the **Grand Palace** (open 10am–6pm; closed Mon and last Tues of the month), and the estate became a hunting park. The palace was later given to Paul I and refashioned by Vincenzo Brenna (1793–97) to resemble a medieval castle, complete with moat and drawbridge. In front of the impressive east facade are the **Upper and Lower Gardens**, which are the wildest of all the palace parks. Of particular interest here are the circular temple of Venus (1792–93), and the Birch House, which looks like a logpile but conceals a palatial suite of mirrored rooms.

In the eastern section of the park on the shore of the Black Lake is the **Priory Palace** (Prioratsky Dvorets; 1799, by Lvov), unique owing to its technical design and reminiscent of a castle from the Middle Ages.

REPINO

About an hour's drive from St Petersburg, on the northern coastal road, is a region of lakes, pine-scented forests and sandy beaches. Here you will find Repino, a resort named after one of Russia's greatest artists, Ilya Repin. He lived on this estate from 1900 to 1930, and his extraordinary *dacha* is now open as a musuem.

Named **Penaty** (open 10.30am–4pm; closed Tues), this is where Repin created many of his masterpieces, including *Pushkin's Examination* and *Bloody Sunday*. You can stroll through the park, visit the studio and get a feel for life at the beginning of the 20th century.

Below: Pavlosk Palace and gardens
Opposite: the Pavlosk State Bedroom

Architecture

Founded in 1703 on a swampy wasteland on the delta of the Neva River, St Petersburg is one of Europe's youngest cities, though it boasts one of the continent's finest architectural legacies. St Petersburg is not only Russia's most European city, but it is perhaps the most European of all Europe's cities. From 1703 until 1917, architects from all over Europe were handsomely paid to build a great capital for the tsars. They had a vast amount of space and a license to systematically create grand buildings where previously there were none. Russian architects also made significant contributions, such as Andrei Zakharov's Admiralty and the Kazan Cathedral, built by the freed serf, Andrei Voronikhin.

STYLE FOLLOWS FASHION

As the years went on and European fashions changed, so did Russian imperial preferences. During Peter's time, as well as during the reign of his daughter, Elisabeth, the Baroque flourished. Structures such as the 12 Collegia and the Catherine Palace (named in honour of Peter's wife) in Tsarskoe Selo are among the most notable.

Catherine the Great, a German princess, loathed what she thought were the extravagancies of the Baroque style and instead preferred the strict facades of Classicism, which were considered to be more in line with Enlightenment ideas on reason. The most prominent buildings of her day include the Tauride Palace, the Marble Palace, and the Russian State Bank (now the Financial and Economics Academy on Griboyedov Canal).

Napolean's defeat at the hands of the alliance led by England and Russia greatly altered St Petersburg's urban landscape, which came to be dominated by triumphal arches, squares for military parades and ceremonial columns. Among these are Palace Square in front of the Hermitage, with its arch of the General Staff Building and the Alexander Column, as well as the Moscow Triumphal Arch on Moskovsky Prospect, Decembrists'

Principal architects
The builders of St Petersburg were given opportunities unheard of in the ancient and crowded cities of Europe. Among them in the 18th and 19th centuries were Italians Francesco Bartolomeo Rastrelli, Antonio Rinaldi, Carlo Rossi, and Giacomo Quarenghi; Swiss architect Domenico Trezzini, Frenchmen Auguste Montferrand and Thomas de Thomon; as well as Englishmen Charles Baird and William Hastie. By the late 19th and early 20th centuries, Scandinavian architects became more prominent, such as the great Swedish art nouveau designer, Fyodor Lidval.

*Opposite: the Admiralty
Bottom: the University*

Below: the Lomonosov Bridge
Bottom: harmonious golden facades

Square and Square of the Arts. The city became famous in Europe for its harmony in style and architecture, earning it the nickname, Palmyr of the North, after the great city in Antiquity.

Architecture often serves the interests of the ruling regime, as well as prevailing social realities. So when Russia gave freedom to its enserfed people in 1861, changes in the city's architecture followed. After this date, few palaces were built in the city, and those that did appear were much smaller. Instead, many apartment houses sprang up to accommodate a growing middle and professional class of lawyers, doctors, and technical specialists. This architectural shift did not compromise quality, but rather redefined it. The city attracted the talents of Scandinavian architects who forged some of the finest works of what is referred to as Historical Style and Northern Art Nouveau, many of which are on the Petrograd Side.

The subsequent move of the capital to Moscow in 1918 was a blessing in disguise, and except for the destruction of World War II – though nearly all buildings were rebuilt in their original appearance – St Petersburg retained its tsarist-era appearance. Even today, city fathers guard their architectural heritage jealously, forbidding any innovation in the city centre that might alter or spoil its grandeur.

Literature

With all its architectural and courtly magnificence, St Petersburg was preordained to evolve into a cultural metropolis par excellence. In terms of having its praises sung, St Petersburg is probably the most literary city in the world. There scarcely exists a Russian writer, no matter where he was born or where he lived, who has not cherished St Petersburg.

Alexander Pushkin, the heart and soul of Russian literature, spent most of his time writing in the city; he loved 'Peter's creation' like nobody else and created an impressive poetic image of the place, which inspired whole chapters of his *Eugene Onegin* (1833). Nicolai Gogol also lived and worked in the city before going abroad, and it was here that he wrote his best works, including *The Government Inspector* (1836).

Although born in Moscow, Fyodor Dostoyevsky wrote almost all his novels in St Petersburg, which he described as 'the most abstract and imaginary city'. His masterpiece, *Crime and Punishment* (1866), is set in St Petersburg's Haymarket district. Leo Tolstoy came to the city on short visits; the English Club is frequently mentioned in *Anna Karenina*.

Music

St Petersburg also evolved into the musical centre of Russia, for it was here that Russian composers tended to create their masterpieces. They include Mikhail Glinka, the unchallenged founder of Russian classical music and author of such brillaint operas as *Ivan Susanin* and *Ruslan and Ludmilla*.

The Russian Musical Society, which introduced regular concerts, was established in St Petersburg in 1859 on the initiative of the composer Anton Rubenstein. Among the first graduates of the conservatoire was Peter Tchaikovsky, one of the greatest, and most prolific, of Russia's symphony and opera composers, creator of such masterpieces as *The Queen of Spades*, and the ballets *Swan Lake*, *The Sleeping Beauty* and *The Nutcracker*.

Ballet

It was at the Mariinsky that Russian ballet came into its own; its resident company still frequently tours abroad. One of its most famous dancers was Anna Pavlova (1881–1931) – responsible for developing the modern *pointe* shoe. She trained at the Imperial Ballet School at the theatre, and in time became its greatest star. Another influential figure that emerged from the St Petersburg ballet scene, was the impressario Serge Diaghilev who set up the Ballets Russe in Paris in 1907. The star dancer of the company was Nijinsky, famous for creating many important roles.

Nijinsky dancing in Le Spectre de la Rose, *1911*

Shostakovich lived in the city and many of his best works were written and premiered here. It was during the 900-day siege that he wrote his *Seventh (Leningrad) Symphony* which was performed at the height of the siege in 1942, the same year that he left. Other great composers whose careers have been closely linked with St Petersburg are Igor Stravinsky and Sergei Prokofiev.

Below: Igor Stravinsky
Bottom: the Yusopov Theatre

Venues

The Mariinsky Opera and Ballet Theatre (known as the Kirov during much of the Communist era) has long enjoyed an international reputation *(see box, page 109)*. But the city has many theatres and auditoriums, both large and small. Here is a list of the main venues. Theatre and concert performances almost always begin at 7pm unless it is a matinee or special event.

Mariinsky Opera and Ballet Theatre, Teatralnaya Ploshchad 1; **Hermitage Theatre**, the State Hermitage Museum; **Yusupov Theatre**, Yusupov Palace; **Aleksandrinsky Theatre**, Ploshchad Ostrovskovo 2; **St Petersburg Opera**, Galernaya Ulitsa 33; **Maly** (small) **Opera Theatre**, Ploshchad Iskusstv 5; **Maly Drama Theatre**, Ulitsa Rubinstein 18; **Gorky Drama Theatre**, Fontanka Embankment 65; **Comedy Theatre**, Nevsky Prospekt 56; **Theatre on the Liteiny**,

Liteiny Prospekt 51; **St Petersburg Philhar-monic Orchestra**, **Bolshoi** (large) **Concert Hall**, Mikhailovskaya Ulitsa 2; **Maly** (small) **Concert Hall**, Nevsky Prospekt 30; **Bolshoi** (large) **Oktyabrsky Concert Hall**, Ligovsky Prospekt 6; **Conservatory Opera Studio**, Teatralnaya Ploshchad 3; **State Cappella Concert Hall**, Moika Embankment 20.

Festivals

St Petersburg spends a good part of the year in cold and darkness, so when the short summer comes, the locals let loose with an intensity rarely seen elsewhere in Europe. During the acclaimed white nights in June, when the sun hardly sets and it never gets dark, the city centre throbs around the clock as people rush to take part in dozens of cultural events in palaces, theatres and museums.

Recent years have seen an explosion of festivals from art and music to film. The central attraction of the white nights is the festival of the same name sponsored by the Mariinsky Opera and Ballet Theatre – **Stars of the White Nights Festival**, which every June features a host of Russian and international stars in opera and ballet. Tickets cost between $50 and $100 and reservations can be made online at the theatre's website: www.mariinsky.ru, but they must be purchased from the box office at Teatralnaya Ploshchad (Square).

Little sister to the Mariinsky's White Nights festival is the annual Chamber Music Festival, **Palaces of St Petersburg**. Featuring international and Russian singers and musicians, among which are those from the Mariinsky Theatre and the St Petersburg Philharmonic, it also runs the entire month of June but is on a much smaller scale, with quartets and soloists performing in the close and intimate quarters of small palace theatres, such as the State Hermitage Theatre, which was the personal theatre of the tsars and tsarinas, the State Russian Museum's Mikhailovksy Palace, the Yusupov Palace, the Marble Palace, as well as the Catherine, Peterhof and Gatchina Palaces, all three located in the city's suburbs.

City Day

St Petersburg's cultural life is certainly steeped in classical arts and culture, but it continues to develop on the popular level. On May 27, City Day, the city commemorates its official founding by Peter the Great in 1703. A flood of parade floats and revelers dressed in costume stream down Nevsky Prospekt, the city's main avenue, to Palace Square next to the Hermitage.

The carnival continues on the first weekend in June with street festivities at the International Tsarsksoe Selo Carnival in the central square of the town. The event includes a wide range of festivities, among which are contests and competitions and the 'cutting of the neckties', a ritual by which the city's bureaucrats are unceremoniously defrocked of their power for one day.

A theatre poster

FOOD AND DRINK

RUSSIAN COOKING

The Russians love hearty meals. For breakfast there is a choice of bread, coffee with milk, tea with lemon, cocoa, sour cream, yoghurt, milk pudding, soft-boiled eggs, omelettes, hot sausages, butter and marmalade. The main meals consist of three or four courses. On offer for the first course are egg dishes, sliced meat or sausage, aspic (with meat, mushrooms or fish), cucumber, prawns, fish salads, brawn, various kinds of fish or black caviar. This is followed by soups, such as *schi* (cabbage soup), *borsch* (beetroot soup with sour cream), *rassolnik* (sausages with gherkins), or meat ball soup; summertime favourites include *akróshka* (cooked meat, smoked sausage, hard-boiled eggs, sliced onion and fresh cucumbers with *kvas* (*see under Drink*), served ice-cold).

For the main dish there is a choice of beef and pork joints, chicken, duck, game, mushrooms, fish (eg. salmon, sturgeon, pike-perch, sterlet) with potatoes, beets, cucumbers, vegetables, salad, and so on. For dessert there are cakes, biscuits, semolina or buckwheat *bliny* (pancakes) with sweet sauces, curd or apples, stewed fruit, *kisyel* (a dish made from fruit juice or fresh berries, dried fruit and potato flour).

Russian cooking is enriched by different regional specialities. From the Ukraine come chicken Kiev and *galushki* (pastry with a meat or curd cheese filling). Also found in St Petersburg are Georgian *shashlik*, Armenian-Turkish *dolma* (minced meat in tomatoes, cucumbers, paprika, etc), *chebureki* (meat pasties) from Central Asia and *pelmeni* (ravioli) from Siberia.

Opposite: the Café de Paris

WHAT TO DRINK

In the drinks line, the big restaurants serve tea, mineral water, fruit juices, beer, vodka, Georgian dry wines, Ukrainian dessert wines, Moldavian and Armenian cognac, Crimean sparkling wine, etc. During the summer *kvas*, a light, fermented drink made out of dried black bread with yeast and raisins, is offered for sale on the street. World-famous of course is Russian vodka. There are various kinds to be recommended: *Russky Standart, Stolichnaya, Zolotoye Koltso, Starorusskaya* and *Sibirskaya*. Soviet champagne is also worth trying, if you can obtain the dry – but expensive – *Sukhoye* variety.

Beer festival

For those ready to let loose altogether, the Annual St Petersburg Beer Festival brings nearly half a million beer lovers, mostly young people, out onto the central streets and squares in mid June. In the 1990s, St Petersburg became Russia's equivalent of Milwaukee, the nation's beer capital, and the country held its first beer festival here in 1996. During the festival, beer lovers can try up to 40 types of Russian beer, such as *Baltika* and *Nevskoye*, and leading Russian pop stars perform at concerts.

WHERE TO EAT

With the great selection of fine restaurants today in the city, it's hard to imagine that not long ago in the mid 1990s, visitors had almost no decent eating option outside their hotel.

The city now has the full range of cafés and restaurants, from quick and cheap to luxurious, that one would expect from any European capital. Finding those restaurants is not always easy, and requires knowing the location ahead of time and having a good map. There is no central culinary strip as in most major cities. Nearly all places accept major credit cards, but you are advised to have the cash on hand just in case the credit card machine is out of order, which is not that uncommon.

Restaurant Selection

Gone are the days of cheap eating, but the city now boasts a varied menu to cater to all tastes and whims. The following restaurants have been subdivided into three categories:
€€€ = expensive, €€ = moderate, € = inexpensive.

RUSSIAN AND EUROPEAN CUISINE

1913 God, Voznesensky Prospekt 13/2, tel: 315-5148. Perhaps the finest Russian cuisine for the price. €€€

Academia, Birzhevoi Proezd 2, tel: 327-8942. Around the corner from the Old Customs House, this restaurant and dance club is quite fashionable with the city's young and rich. The pizza is quite good. €€€

Akvarel, Prospekt Dobrulyubova 14a, tel: 320-8600, Good food, and great view on the embankment; young, fashionable crowd. €€€

Austeria, Peter and Paul Fortress, tel: 238-4262. Atmosphere of early St Petersburg, with fine Russian and European cuisine. €€€

Bliny Domik, Kolokolnaya Ulitsa 8, tel: 315-9915. Cheap, great Russian food with artsy atmosphere. €.

Borsalino, Angleterre Hotel, Bolshaya Morskaya 39, tel: 313-5115. Decent European cuisine. €€€

Crocodile, Galernaya Ulitsa 18, tel: 314-9437. Cult café for local bohemian circles. Great food and cool atmosphere. €

Idiot, Naberezhnaya Reki Moiki 82, tel: 315-1675. Great atmosphere, great cappuccino, and good vegetarian meals. €

Kameya, 2nd Sovetskaya 21, tel: 277-5542. Russian cuisine in quiet, elegant atmosphere, off the beaten track. €€€

Laima, Nevsky Prospekt 30/16, tel: 315-5545. Modern bistro. €

ME 100, 18 Ulitsa Lenin (Petrograd Side), tel: 230-5359. Russian, Japanese and Italian cuisine. Small and stylish restaurant. Great food at probably the best price in town. Friendly, English-speaking owner, Katya, almost always on premises. €€€

Na Zdorovye, Bolshoi Prospekt 13, tel: 232-4039. Good Russian food in folksy, kitschy interior. €€

The Noble Nest, Dekabristov Ulitsa 21, tel: 312-3205. The city's most expensive and elite location, with tsarist grandeur. €€€

Old Customs House, Tamozheny Pereulok 1, tel: 327-8980. Just across the street from Restoran, this restaurant is Russian-owned, but British run. Excellent European and Russian cuisine, but pretentious. €€€

Onegin, Sadovaya Ulitsa 11, tel: 311-8384. Exquisite French and Russian cuisine, and pricey. Exclusive club frequented by local celebrities. DJ late night. €€€

Propaganda, Naberezhnaya Reki Fontanki 40, tel: 275-3558. Fashionable café that exploits the Soviet theme, at socialist prices. €

Restoran, Tamozheny Pereulok 2, tel: 327-8979. Just across from the Ethnological Museum (Kunstkamera). Restoran's sleek and cold simplicity, with elements of pre-1917 Russian tastes, was designed by one of the country's leading interior designers, Andrei Dmitriev. €€€

Russkaya Ribalka, Uzhnaya Doroga 11, tel: 323-9813. The best fish dinner, and where you can catch your own fish in their pond. Far from the centre, located on the Krestovsky Island on the Petrograd Side. **€€**

Shinok, Zagorodny Prospekt 13; tel: 311-8262. Excellent Ukrainian food served in village interior; also features live music in the evenings. **€€€**

St Petersburg, Kanal Griboyedov 5, tel: 314-4947. Fine Russian cuisine. **€€€**

Staroe Café, Fontanka Embankment 108, tel: 316-5111. With only four tables, the Old Café makes for a very romantic and cosy evening, with good Russian cuisine. The décor features genuine antiques from the late 19th century. After 7pm, a piano player hits out some tunes. **€€**

Tinkoff, Ulitsa Kazanskaya 7, tel: 118-5566. Hip club and restaurant. Great salads, pizza and sushi. Has own microbrewery. **€€**

Troitsky Most, Malaya Posadksaya Ulitsa 4, Kronvergsky Prospekt 29, tel: 232-6693. The best buy in town. Fine and original vegetarian cooking. **€**

Valhalla, Nevsky Prospekt 22, tel: 311-0024. A hearty Russian dinner on Nevsky Prospekt for those looking for a rowdy night out. **€€€**

Zov Ilicha (Lenin's Mating Call), Kazanskaya Ulitsa 34, tel: 117-8641. The interior is a great parody on the Soviet era, but at capitalist prices. Russian and French cuisine. **€€€**

CHINESE

Golden Dragon, Dekabristov Ulitsa 62, tel: 114-8441. Around 120 Chinese dishes to choose from. **€€**

Golden Dragon By the Zoo, Kronverksky Prospekt 61, tel: 232-2643. Fine Chinese cuisine in quiet, charming atmosphere. **€€**

JEWISH

Sem Sorok, Bolshoi Samsonievsky 108, tel: 246-3444. **€€€**

Shalom, Ulitsa Koly Tomchaka, 8A, tel: 327-5475. **€€€**

CAUCASIAN

Kavkaz Bar, Karavannaya Ulitsa 18, tel: 312-1665. Exotic Caucasion interior and fine shish kebabs. **€€€**

Ketino, 8th Line 23, Vasilevsky Island, tel: 326-0196. Exquisite Georgian cooking, but not cheap. Fine collection of Georgian art on display. **€€**

Salkhino, Kronversky Prospekt 25, tel: 232-7891. Great Georgian cooking, but not cheap. Laura Bush ate here. **€€**

ITALIAN

Macaroni, Rubinstein Ulitsa 23, tel: 315-6147. One of the few fine Italian restaurants in the city. **€€**

*The cosy interior of
the Café Idiot*

Nightlife

St Petersburg boasts a wide range of exciting nightlife. Techno clubs are very popular with young people, but there is also a good choice of Russian folk shows. There is also a vibrant underground culture, especially cabarets and informal theatres. Please note that most clubs have club cards and/or strict face control, but foreigners are rarely turned away.

Chaplin Club, Ulitsa Chaikovskogo 59, tel: 272-6649. City's best comedy club. Some shows are mime; but most in Russian.

Comic Trust. Homeless underground comedy theatre that uses no language, but music, gestures, and mimicry. This outrageous theatre is the other, St. Petersburg, far from the high culture of the Mariinksy Theatre. Check their website for shows: www.comic-trust.com

Jakata, Prospekt Bakunin 5, tel: 346-7461. Two dance floors, and good food; among most fashionable clubs.

Jet Set, Furshtatskaya Ulitsa 58b, tel: 275-9288. Face-control and club cards. Sumptuous eastern-style interior, and resident European DJs.

Onegin, Sadovaya Ulitsa, tel: 117-8384. Home to the city's most fashionable and beautiful crowd.

Par.SPb, Alexandrovsky Park 5b, tel: 233-3374. Techno club, popular with foreigners.

Plaza, Naberezhnaya Makarov 2, tel: 323-9090. Upscale and expensive disco, popular with foreigners.

Purga, Naberezhnaya Reki Fontanki 13, tel: 313-4123. Very popular; New Year's Eve is celebrated every night.

Prival.Com, Corner of Naberezhnaya Reki Moiki and Marsovaya Polye, tel: 314-3849. Pre-1917 Bohemian hang-out in basement. Good food and fun shows on weekends.

Stray Dog, Ploshchad Isskusstv 5, tel: 315-7764. Historic club that originally opened in 1912 and was centre of Silver Age artists. Art exhibits and musical performances, plus dining.

Tunnel, In a bunker at the corner of Zverinsky and Lyubanksy Pereulok, tel: 233-4015. Student club.

Mama Roma's, Karavannaya Ulitsa 3, tel: 314-0347. A step above the typical pizzeria. €€

Patio Pizza, Nevsky Prospekt 30, tel: 314-8215. Good pizza, centrally located. €€

Pizzacato, Bolshaya Morskaya 45, tel: 315-0319. Also very good pizza, but it's in the basement. €€

OTHER RESTAURANTS

Bistro Garçon, Nevsky Prospekt 95, tel: 277-2467. Fine French cuisine in cosy Parisian setting. €€€

Brasilia, Kazanskaya Street 24, tel: 320-8777. Popular with the young and affluent, this features Latin-style food and exotic cocktails in a sexy, stylish atmosphere. €€€

Caravan, Voznesensky Prospekt, tel: 310-5678. Excellent Central Asian food in motif interior. €€€

Marius Pub, Ulitsa Marata 11, tel: 315-4880. Traditional Swiss pub with fine German fare. One of the few places that is open 24 hours. €€

Coffee Houses

Che, Poltavskaya Ulitsa 3, tel: 277-7600. Coolest café in city, with live jazz music daily.

Marko, Nevsky Prospekt 16 and 108, tel: 275-7559. Good coffee, a variety of salads and great desserts. Also, place for students.

Marrakesh, Karavannaya Ulitsa 3, tel: 117-8047. Exquisite teahouse for upscale and fashionable crowd.

Bars, Pubs and Beer Halls

Korsar, Bolshaya Morskaya 14, tel: 318-4184. A varied programme of live music and themed entertainment.

Mollie's Irish Pub, Rubinstein Ulitsa 36, tel: 319-9768. One of the livelier bars, serving draught Guinness, numerous other beers, and pub food.

Shamrock, Dekabristov Ulitsa 27, tel: 318-4625. Another popular Irish bar.

SHOPPING

The best-known souvenir from Russia is a Matrioshka doll. Painted wooden spoons, lacquered boxes and brooches are also popular. Other items include: wood carvings; china from the Lomonosov porcelain factory; tableware; gaily painted toys made of clay; embroidered, knitted and leather articles; records with Russian folk or classical music; head scarves from Orenburg and Pavlov-Posad; and of course Russian caviar.

SOUVENIRS AND ART

Most of these souvenir items can be purchased in the shops of the **Grand Hotel Europe**, **Kareliya**, **St Petersburg**, **Pribaltiskaya** and **Sovyetskaya**. But these places are expensive, so you may prefer to try out the **Souvenir Market** next to the Saviour on the Blood Church. On Nevsky Prospekt, in front of the Catholic Church of St Catherine, is an artists' colony.

FOOD MARKETS

There are 16 so-called collective markets where farmers sell fruit, vegetables and other food products from different regions of Russia. The biggest and best include: **Kuznechny**, Kuznetschny Pereulok 3; **Andreyevsky**, Vasilievsky Ostrov, 18 Bolshoi Prospekt; and **Sytny**, 3/5 Sytninskaya Ploshchad. Watch out for the games salespeople play.

SHOPS

Warehouses and department stores: DLT, Bolshaya Konyushennaya 21/3; **Gostiny Dvor**, Nevsky Prospekt 7/9; **Passage**, Nevsky Prospekt 48.

Antiques: **Russkaya Starina**, Nevsky Prospekt 20; **Lomanny Grosh**, Mokhovaya Ulitsa 31; **Larusse**, Stremyanaya Street 3.

Bookshops: **Dom Knigi** (House of Books), Nevsky Prospekt 28; **Technicheskaya Kniga**, Liteiny Prospekt 57.

Gifts: **Onegin Art Store**, Italyanskaya Ulitsa 11; **Stroganov Palace Art Store**, Nevsky Prospekt 17; **Grand Palace**, Nevsky Prospekt 21–23; **Passage**, Nevsky Prospekt 48.

Gourmet Food: **Yeliseyevsky Gastronom**, Nevsky Prospekt 56.

Jewellery: **Samosvety**, Mikhailovskaya Ulitsa 6; **Yakhont**, Bolshaya Morskaya Ulitsa 24; **Agat**, Sadovaya Ulitsa 47.

Fur is still worn in Russia

PRACTICAL INFORMATION

Getting There

BY AIR

There are five weekly flights from London with British Airways and three weekly flights with Aeroflot. There are also four weekly flights from London with Scandinavian Airlines via Copenhagen and with Austrian Airlines via Vienna. The plane journey from London takes about three and a half hours, or about six hours with a stopover in a European city. Delta Airlines runs connecting flights from major European capitals. Planes arrive at the Pulkovo Airport, which is 17km (10½ miles) from the city centre; a shuttle service is available. There is a regular Aeroflot service between Moscow and St Petersburg (almost every hour).

BY TRAIN

Trains coming in from western Europe arrive at Warsaw Station. The journey takes 33 hours from Berlin and 48 hours from Paris. The Finland Station caters for traffic from the north; trains from Helsinki arrive here (via Vyborg, the trip takes about 7 hours). Trains from Moscow arrive at the Moscow Station and the journey from Moscow to St Petersburg takes 7 to 8 hours.

BY BOAT

Arriving in St Petersburg by boat can be one of the most exciting ways to approach the city. However, cruises and ferries operate irregularly, so it is best to check with a travel agent for details *(see page 122)*. Passenger ships arrive in St Petersburg from the following cities: London, Bremerhaven, Helsinki, Copenhagen, Göteborg, Stockholm, Montreal and New York; they dock at the Seaport Passenger

Finland connection
The VR Passenger Service offers two trains a day between Helsinki and St Petersburg, departing at 6.56am and 3.34pm. The journey takes around 6½ hours. For further information, log on to their website, www.vr.fi; bookings can be made through the UK-based agency Freedom Rail (tel: 01252-728506; www.freedomrail.co.uk).

Terminal, located at the southeastern tip of Vasilievsky Island. If you arrive by cruise ship, you do not need a visa, provided you spend every night on board your cruise ship.

BY CAR

Driving to St Petersburg has the advantage of making it easier to visit the beautiful surroundings of the city on the Neva, as well as giving you a better impression of some of the Russian countryside.

Driving from western Europe, the shortest route is from either Germany or the Czech Republic through Poland. From the Polish-Belorussian border at Brest one can proceed either via Minsk, Orsha and Vitebsk (in Belorussia), and on to Pskov and St Petersburg; or via Minsk, Smolensk and Moscow. St Petersburg can also be approached by car from Finland – the city is only 218km (135 miles) from the Finnish border.

Details of cars must be entered on your visa. Motorists who present their national driving licence at the border will be asked to complete a driving licence insert so that the information on the licence can be understood by the Russian authorities. Visitors who are intending to stay in Russia for longer than a month should obtain an international driving licence. All foreign cars must show a nationality plate. There is no obligatory Third Party Liability and the Green Card or international insurance certificate does not apply.

St Petersburg now boasts new service and repair stations for non-Russian cars. But you should still be cautious of the state of Russian roads. Diverting from the highways may get you into some unexpected adventures. Accommodation and petrol stations are few and far between, and you may find that you are only allowed to stay at pre-booked hotels or campsites along your planned route. It is therefore recommended that you organise your journey through a recognised travel agency.

Further information can be obtained from Western automobile associations, Intourist and other specialist travel agencies *(see page 122)*. Compared to Western countries, traffic is light.

Travel Within Russia

BY TRAIN

As a traditional mode of transport, the railway, partly modernised with electricity and partly diesel, still plays an important role in national transport.

Facilities in the normal trains are good, in the express trains excellent.

The transcontinental rail routes (such as those from Moscow to Vladivostok) demand an adventurous spirit and a week spent in the train contemplating the endless Siberian landscapes. Food should be taken along since station buffet food is often not to the liking of weary travellers. Since train journeys are in great demand and the trains are often full, it is wise to book and pay for tickets at least two days before departure.

BY AIR

Within the Russian Federation, a busy flight network connects the most important cities. Inland there is only one flight class. Compared to the prices paid by western Europeans for the same distances at home, Russian flights are relatively cheap. Apart from Moscow, there are direct flights from St Petersburg to Sochi and Volgograd (Russia), Kiev, Kharkov, Odessa (Ukraine), Minsk (Belarus), Vilnius (Lithuania), Yerevan (Armenia), Tbilisi (Georgia) and other towns. Note that each state requires a separate visa.

Public transport is efficient and cheap

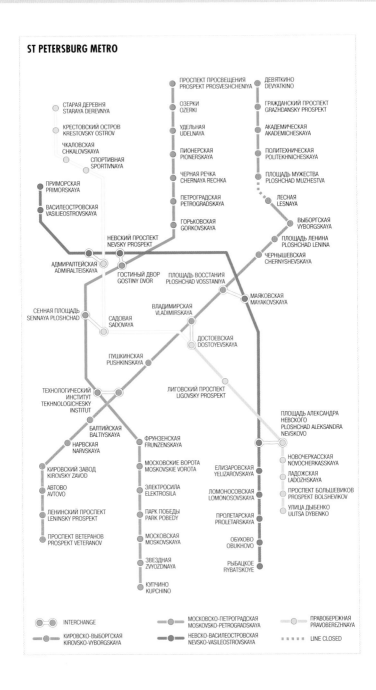

ST PETERSBURG METRO

СТАРАЯ ДЕРЕВНЯ
STARAYA DEREVNYA

КРЕСТОВСКИЙ ОСТРОВ
KRESTOVSKY OSTROV

ЧКАЛОВСКАЯ
CHKALOVSKAYA

СПОРТИВНАЯ
SPORTIVNAYA

ПРИМОРСКАЯ
PRIMORSKAYA

ВАСИЛЕОСТРОВСКАЯ
VASILIEOSTROVSKAYA

НЕВСКИЙ ПРОСПЕКТ
NEVSKY PROSPEKT

АДМИРАЛТЕЙСКАЯ
ADMIRALTEISKAYA

ГОСТИНЫЙ ДВОР
GOSTINY DVOR

СЕННАЯ ПЛОЩАДЬ
SENNAYA PLOSHCHAD

САДОВАЯ
SADOVAYA

ПУШКИНСКАЯ
PUSHKINSKAYA

ТЕХНОЛОГИЧЕСКИЙ
ИНСТИТУТ
TEKHNOLOGICHESKY
INSTITUT

БАЛТИЙСКАЯ
BALTIYSKAYA

НАРВСКАЯ
NARVSKAYA

КИРОВСКИЙ ЗАВОД
KIROVSKY ZAVOD

АВТОВО
AVTOVO

ЛЕНИНСКИЙ ПРОСПЕКТ
LENINSKY PROSPEKT

ПРОСПЕКТ ВЕТЕРАНОВ
PROSPEKT VETERANOV

ПРОСПЕКТ ПРОСВЕЩЕНИЯ
PROSPEKT PROSVESHCHENIYA

ОЗЕРКИ
OZERKI

УДЕЛЬНАЯ
UDELNAYA

ПИОНЕРСКАЯ
PIONERSKAYA

ЧЕРНАЯ РЕЧКА
CHERNAYA RECHKA

ПЕТРОГРАДСКАЯ
PETROGRADSKAYA

ГОРЬКОВСКАЯ
GORKOVSKAYA

ПЛОЩАДЬ ВОССТАНИЯ
PLOSHCHAD VOSSTANIYA

ВЛАДИМИРСКАЯ
VLADIMIRSKAYA

ДОСТОЕВСКАЯ
DOSTOYEVSKAYA

ЛИГОВСКИЙ ПРОСПЕКТ
LIGOVSKY PROSPEKT

ФРУНЗЕНСКАЯ
FRUNZENSKAYA

МОСКОВСКИЕ ВОРОТА
MOSKOVSKIE VOROTA

ЭЛЕКТРОСИЛА
ELEKTROSILA

ПАРК ПОБЕДЫ
PARK POBEDY

МОСКОВСКАЯ
MOSKOVSKAYA

ЗВЕЗДНАЯ
ZVYOZDNAYA

КУПЧИНО
KUPCHINO

ЕЛИЗАРОВСКАЯ
YELIZAROVSKAYA

ЛОМОНОСОВСКАЯ
LOMONOSOVSKAYA

ПРОЛЕТАРСКАЯ
PROLETARSKAYA

ОБУХОВО
OBUKHOVO

РЫБАЦКОЕ
RYBATSKOYE

ДЕВЯТКИНО
DEVYATKINO

ГРАЖДАНСКИЙ ПРОСПЕКТ
GRAZHDANSKY PROSPEKT

АКАДЕМИЧЕСКАЯ
AKADEMICHESKAYA

ПОЛИТЕХНИЧЕСКАЯ
POLITEKHNICHESKAYA

ПЛОЩАДЬ МУЖЕСТВА
PLOSHCHAD MUZHESTVA

ЛЕСНАЯ
LESNAYA

ВЫБОРГСКАЯ
VYBORGSKAYA

ПЛОЩАДЬ ЛЕНИНА
PLOSHCHAD LENINA

ЧЕРНЫШЕВСКАЯ
CHERNYSHEVSKAYA

МАЯКОВСКАЯ
MAYAKOVSKAYA

ПЛОЩАДЬ АЛЕКСАНДРА
НЕВСКОГО
PLOSHCHAD ALEKSANDRA
NEVSKOVO

НОВОЧЕРКАССКАЯ
NOVOCHERKASSKAYA

ЛАДОЖСКАЯ
LADOZHSKAYA

ПРОСПЕКТ БОЛЬШЕВИКОВ
PROSPEKT BOLSHEVIKOV

УЛИЦА ДЫБЕНКО
ULITSA DYBENKO

Legend

INTERCHANGE

КИРОВСКО-ВЫБОРГСКАЯ
KIROVSKO-VYBORGSKAYA

МОСКОВСКО-ПЕТРОГРАДСКАЯ
MOSKOVSKO-PETROGRADSKAYA

НЕВСКО-ВАСИЛЕОСТРОВСКАЯ
NEVSKO-VASILEOSTROVSKAYA

ПРАВОБЕРЕЖНАЯ
PRAVOBEREZHNAYA

LINE CLOSED

Getting Around

METRO (UNDERGROUND)

The signs and underground maps with lighted routes make it possible to find the right direction quickly *(see map)*. Tokens are bought at the ticket office and these are fed into the automatic barriers. The Metro runs from 5.30am until 12.30am.

TAXIS

Taxis have a cap on top of the car and are usually yellow. The green light on the windscreen is on if the taxi is free. Today, many private car owners also provide a taxi service, although it's best to stick to licensed cabs. If you do take a private taxi, negotiate the fare before your journey, as these cars do not have a meter. Dvuch Stolits, tel: 928-0000, city centre to airport 600 rubles. Severnaya Palmira, tel: 312-6300, city centre to airport 450 rubles. Taxi Blues, tel: 271-8888, city centre to airport 450 rubles.

HIRE CARS

In St Petersburg and other large cities you can hire a car as long as you have an international driving licence. Further information about the different cars available and current hire charges can be obtained from the Intourist service offices in most hotels. Petrol and car-washing costs are the responsibility of the person hiring the car. It is also possible to hire a car with a local driver, and this can be arranged through the same channels. Hertz, Malaya Morskaya Ulitsa 23, tel: 324-3242; www.hertz.spb.ru

TRAFFIC POLICE

Traffic police can be recognised by their white belts and shoulder straps. Their cars are distinguishable by the blue horizontal strips and three large characters on the bodywork. Known

Raising the drawbridge

From early April to early November, St Petersburg's drawbridges along the Neva River rise each night at around 1.45am, and stay up until almost 5am, as freighters and tankers travel up and downstream. The sight is one of the most unforgettable in the world, but it also creates inconvenience for nightlife if you're trying to get to a club or get home. If you don't cross at 1.45am, there is one bridge, the Palace Bridge (Dvortsovy Most) next to the Hermitage, which descends at 2.45am for about 20 minutes to let cars across.

by their initials GIBDD, the traffic police are notoriously corrupt and extort money from drivers for both real and imagined violations. Failure to pay may result in confiscation of your licence and car.

BY TROLLEYBUS, TRAM AND BUS

The services run from 5.30am until midnight. On all forms of public transport you are unlikely to get a seat during the day, and queuing to get on is rare, so be prepared for the crush. A flat fare is payable, whatever the length of the journey; you buy a ticket from the conductor, who wears a red armband, or from the driver.

The No 10 trolleybus is good for sightseeing, running from Ploshchad Aleksandra Nevskovo through the centre and across Vasilievsky Island.

BY BOAT

From May to October it is possible to view the city from a steamer on the Neva (departure points: Decembrists' Square, Palace Square or the Embankment by the Summer Garden); or you can take a river trip to Peterhof (departure point: Palace Embankment at the Hermitage). Water taxis are also available during the warmer months, and can carry anything from four to 20 people. For further information, ask your travel agent *(see page 122)*.

ON FOOT

Anyone lucky enough to be in St Petersburg for the White Nights in June, when the sun hardly sets, should have a wander around one evening (along with what seems like all the city's inhabitants). Begin at Dvortsovaya Ploshchad (Palace Square), walk along Millionnaya Ulitsa (Millionaire's Street) to Zimnyaya Kanavka (Winter Canal), then left to Dvortsovaya Naberezhnaya (Palace Embankment), along to Dvortsovy Most (Palace Bridge) and across the Neva to Birzhevaya Ploshchad (Stock Exchange Square) on the Strelka spit. The view from this spot, over one of the most beautiful parts of the city, is impressive.

Glossary
ulitsa street
bulvar boulevard
prospekt avenue
ploshchad square
pereulok lane, small street
naberezhnaya embankment
ostrov island
storona district
dom house
most bridge
vokzal train station

Facts for the Visitor

TRAVEL DOCUMENTS

A visitor to Russia must have a valid passport and visa. The easiest way to obtain a visa is through a travel agent *(see below)*. A tourist visa is valid for between 10 and 30 days, and varies in price depending on how quickly it is needed. On the visa are the date and place of arrival and departure as well as the length of the trip. Changes are only possible in conjunction with an

Carry your passport
According to Russian law, everyone should carry his or her passport (Russians have an internal one) at all times. Foreigners also need to carry a visa. Some choose to carry photocopies of these, fearing they may be stolen, as it is extremely difficult to replace your visa if lost or stolen. But police don't always accept photocopies as valid. Be wary of the police, especially at night, as they often shake down citizens and tourists.

Intourist office. It is only possible to extend a trip to St Petersburg after arrival. In order to obtain a visa, the travel agency will require a valid passport, visa application form and one passport photograph. If you apply individually you will need confirmation of hotel reservations. Applications should be made at least one month before departure.

CUSTOMS

Antiques and manuscripts may not be exported. Items for personal use when travelling, such as personal computers, cameras, video cameras with film, tape recorders and portable musical instruments are permitted. Note that all precious metals such as wedding rings must be declared on arrival.

EXCHANGE REGULATIONS

Foreign currency and other forms of currency such as travellers' cheques may be imported, but must be declared upon arrival on a customs declaration form. Currency taken out of the country must not exceed the amount shown on the import declaration, which you will need to present when leaving the country. Importing and exporting Russian notes and coins is prohibited.

TRAVEL AGENTS

Tickets, by rail or air, to any city in

Russia and the Commonwealth of Independent States can be purchased at any travel agency. There are plenty to choose from, among which are:

Eclectica Guide, Nevsky Prospekt 44, tel: 110-5579; gid@eclectica.spb.ru Specialises in tours of St. Petersburg and its suburbs.

Intourist St Petersburg Ltd, 11 Isaakiyevskaya Ploshchad, tel: 812-315 5129. **MIR International Centre** 45 Voronezhskaya, tel: 812-167 0831, fax: 812-167 1830.

Lenart Tours, Nevsky Prospekt 40, tel: 312-6553; www.lenart.spb.ru

Wild Russia, Naberezhnaya Reki Fontanki 58, tel: 313-8030; www.wildrussia.spb.ru Specialises in tourism to wilderness areas.

WHAT'S ON

Information on events, concerts, bookings, etc, can be found in English-language papers such as the *St Petersburg Times* and *Pulse*.

CURRENCY AND EXCHANGE

Roubles cannot be obtained outside Russia, but all major hotels have an official exchange counter, where you can buy them with cash, travellers' cheques or credit cards. In addition, there are *bureaux de change* through-

> ### Intourist
> Intourist, the former state travel agency, was privatised in 1993. Although it no longer has a monopoly on Russian travel, it continues to offer services in all the larger Russian cities and, with its huge network of offices and agents, remains by far the largest travel company in the country. Intourist runs numerous hotels, motels, campsites and restaurants, organises sightseeing trips and conducted tours, and arranges the hire of cars, coaches and minibuses. Besides group tours, Intourist also arranges for individual journeys to Russia.

out the city, many of which can be found in the larger shops. You will be asked to present your passport and visa. Make sure you keep the receipts from any exchange transaction, as you will need to attach them to the customs declaration form on your departure *(see page 122)*.

TIPPING

The recommended amount is 5–10 percent of the invoiced amount. Watch out for waiters and waitresses who do not return your change.

OPENING TIMES

Offices: Monday to Friday 9am–6pm. *Food shops:* Monday to Saturday 8am–1pm and 2–9pm, Sunday 8am–1pm and 2–6pm. *Other shops:* Monday to Saturday 11am–2pm and 3–9pm.

PHOTOGRAPHY

Photographic equipment is easily obtained and there are quick film-developing services. Most hotels sell photographic equipment. Generally speaking, taking photographs in galleries, museums and exhibitions is permitted, though often at a charge.

PUBLIC HOLIDAYS AND FESTIVALS

1 January (New Year's Day); 7 January (Orthodox Christmas); 23 February (Defender's Day); 8 March (Women's Day); 1–2 May (May Holiday); 9 May (VE Day); 12 June (Independence Day); 7 November (Day of Reconciliation); 12 December (Constitution Day).

St Petersburg's main festive season is during the acclaimed White Nights, when the sun barely sets, and it never quite gets dark. During this period there are concerts, opera and ballet performances throughout the city. The most popular place to be at night is on the banks of the Neva at around 1.45am, when the bridges are raised *(see page 121)*.

POST OFFICES, TELEPHONES

Main post office (Glavny Pochtant): Pochstamskaya Ulitsa 9, (8am–10pm); every large hotel has a post office with facilities for basic postal services. Post offices usually open at 10am, but routine postal services are available at the reception area in the larger hotels between 8am–8pm.

Central telephone and telegraph office: Pochantskaya Ulitsa 9. Local calls may be made from hotels at no charge, but making an international call from a hotel can be expensive. There are public phone booths all over the city, and you can call abroad from many of them ('International'). The phones take phone cards which are available from post offices or Metro ticket offices. To make an international call, dial 8 + 10 + the international code of the country you are dialling (US 1; UK 44).

TIME DIFFERENCE

St Petersburg time is three hours ahead of Greenwich Mean Time. In summer the clock is put forward an hour.

ELECTRICITY

The standard voltage in Russia is 220 AC. Sockets require continental adaptors.

MEDICAL

There's no reason to fear medical treatment in Russia. There are a number of fine western clinics with the most modern medicine and the best Russian doctors, well versed in both western and eastern medical traditions. Rates are not cheap, but less than market rates in the West.

American Medical Clinic, Nagerezhnaya Reki Moiki 78, tel: 140-2090; www.amclinic.com English-speaking doctors; open 24 hours.

British-American Family Practice, Grafsky Pereulok 7, tel: 327-6030; www.british-americanclinic.com Full-time British GP and English-speaking Russian doctors; open 24 hours.

International Clinic, Ulitsa Dostoyevkovo 19, tel: 320-3870; www.icspb.com English-speaking Russian doctors.

Dental Services, Medi, Nevsky Prospekt 82, tel: 324-0000; www.emedi.ru The city's best dental clinic. Open 24 hours.

LOST PROPERTY

Sacharievskaya Ulitsa 19, tel: 278-3690; Vasilievsky Ostrov 70 Sredny Prospekt, tel: 213-0039.

LOCAL ETTIQUETTE

Russians can be quite robustly vocal, and sometimes appear to be angry when in fact they are having an everyday conversation. So don't worry if you came across a shouting match.

Safety

If you are only in the city for pleasure, there is little reason to worry about your physical safety, provided you take the same precautions you would while walking in any major city. These include keeping valuables hidden and avoiding unlit streets.

Women should be aware that Russian men can be aggressive, and their attitude towards them is old-fashioned at best, sexist at worst. If a Russian woman in a restaurant or bar comes across as forward, she may be a prostitute.

Foreigners are more likely to be victimised by the police (*militsiya*) than by street thugs. The Russian police are notoriously corrupt, and have ties to criminal groups. Attacks most often happen late at night. The police usually wait near nightclubs and bars, and prey on those coming out, especially when more than a little tipsy. Russian law requires you carry your passport, and if police catch you without one, they have the right to detain you for several days. Avoid the police after dark. If cornered, demand that you want to call your consulate.

ACCOMMODATION

BED SHORTAGES

The ever-increasing stream of foreign tourists, which has reached about 2½ million a year, is flowing into a small supply of hotel space. It is almost impossible to find rooms during the peak months of June and July. The city has about 130 private and state-owned hotels with 32,000 beds, but a fair number are pretty basic. For most of the 1990s, visitors only had about five decent hotels to choose from. The city's 300th anniversary, however, stimulated a boom in hotel construction, especially small guesthouses and B&Bs.

Some visitors get around the hotel problem by sailing into St Petersburg on a cruise liner, which indeed do bring the majority of foreign tourists into the city during the summer.

Hotel Selection

The hotels are divided into three categories: €€€ = expensive, €€ = moderate, € = inexpensive.

€€€

Angleterre Hotel, Bolshaya Morskaya Ulitsa 39, tel: 313-5666, fax: 313-5125; e-mail: reservation@angleterre-hotel.spb.ru; www.angleterrehotel.com Owned by the same company as the Astoria, in an adjacent building on St Isaac's Square, but less expensive.

Astoria Hotel, Bolshaya Morskaya Ulitsa 39, tel: 313-5757, fax: 313-5134; e-mail: reserve@astoria.spb.ru; www.roccofortehotels.com Centrally located on St Isaac's Square with a view of the cathedral, this is one of the city's most luxurious hotels.

Grand Hotel Europe, Mikhailovskaya Ulitsa 7, tel: 329-6000, fax: 329-6001; e-mail: hotel@ghe.spb.ru; www. grandhoteleurope.com With elegant decor and refined service, this luxury hotel is the most expensive in the city and, since its renovation in 1991, has set the standard for all St Petersburg hotels to emulate. Near the Russian Museum just off Nevsky Prospekt.

Kazansky Hotel, Ulitsa Kazanskaya 5, tel: 327-7466, 327-7467; www.kazansky5.com Small exquisite, upscale hotel in heart of city, furnished with genuine antique furniture.

Radisson SAS Royal Hotel, Nevsky Prospekt 49, tel: 322-5000, fax: 322-5002; e-mail: stpetersburg@radissonsas.com; www.radissonsas.com Centrally located on the city's main thoroughfare, the Radisson is one of the city's newer hotels.

Sheraton Nevsky Palace, Nevsky Prospekt 57, tel: (812) 275-2001, fax: (812) 301-7323; e-mail: bc@sheraton nevskij.ru Characterised by sparse, modern interiors, the Sheraton has good restaurants and business facilities.

€€

Hotel Dostoyevsky, Vladimirsky Prospekt 19, tel: 331-3200, fax: 331-3201; e-mail: info@dostoevsky-hotel.ru; www.vladimirskiy.ru This is a good three star option, with comfortable rooms in a well-run hotel.

Hotel Moskva, Ploshchad Alexandra Nevskogo 2, tel: 274-0022, 274-2052, fax: 274-2130; e-mail: business@hotel-moscow.ru; www.hotel-moscow.ru A Soviet-style hotel well located on the river, opposite the Alexander Nevsky monastery and near the metro station.

Oktyabrsky Hotel, Ligovsky Prospekt 10, tel: 277-6330, fax: 315-7501; e-mail: hotel@oktober.spb.ru; www. oktober-hotel.spb.ru Built in 1847, this hotel shows some remnants of its former glory; try and book one of the renovated rooms.

Pribaltiskaya Hotel, Ulitsa Korable-stroiteley 14, tel: 356-3001, 356-2157, fax: 356-6094; e-mail: market@pribaltiyskaya.ru; www.pribaltiyskaya.ru A modern high-rise popular with package tour groups and far from the city centre; however, it does have stunning views overlooking the Gulf of Finland.

Hotel St Petersburg, Pirogovskaya Naberezhnaya 5, tel: 380-1919, fax: 380-1920; e-mail: reservation@hotel-spb.ru; www.hotel-spb.ru Although this hotel has not been renovated since Soviet times (and thus has a distinctly 'period charm' to the rooms), it has a great view of the river in the city centre.

€

Neptune Hotel and Business Centre, Nab Obvodny Kanal 93A, tel: (812) 324-2000, fax: (812) 324-4611; e-mail: hotel@neptune.spb.ru; www.neptune.spb.ru Popular with business travellers, as the Neptune is clean and efficient.

Sovetskaya Hotel, Lermontovsky Prospekt 43, tel: (812) 329-0182, fax: (812) 251-8890; e-mail: hotel@sovetskaya.com; www.sovetskaya.com Living up to its name, with some rooms quite Soviet in decor and service. However, it is good value. Book into the Riga Building (12th and 14th floors, reserved for visitors).

Apartments

Alexander House, Naberezhnaya Krukov Canal 27, tel: (812) 259-6877; e-mail: info@a-house.ru; www.a-house.ru Luxurious four-star apartments at three-star prices. Best for long stays. Close to Mariinsky Theatre.

Pulford Real Estate, tel: (812) 325-6277, fax: (812) 320-7561; e-mail: pulford@mail.wplus.net; www.pulford.com Many residents like to rent out their apartment for hard currency. This can be a personal and inexpensive way of staying in the city for longer periods, and avoiding the Intourist hotel charges.

Bed and Breakfast/Mini-hotels

Rand House (www.randhouse.ru): Bolshaya Morskaya Ulitsa 25, Flat 17 (3rd floor), tel: 314-6333. Grivtsova Lane 11, Flat 83 (4th floor), tel: 310-7005. Admiralteyskaya Embankment 6, Flats 19 and 20, tel: 312-7152. Sadovaya Street 11, Flat 50 (3rd floor), tel: 315-1037. A well-run, American chain with budget accommodation. **€**

Comfort Hotel, Bolshaya Morskaya Ulitsa 25, tel: 314-6523, fax: 318-6700; e-mail: info@comfort-hotel.ru; www.comfort-hotel.spb.ru A good, clean budget option. **€**

Youth Hostels

International Hostel Holiday, Ulitsa Mikhailova 1, tel: 327-1070, fax: 327-1033; e-mail: info@hostel.spb.ru; www.hostel.ru Popular with Russian visitors, this hostel is near the Finland train station.

St Petersburg International Youth Hostel, 3rd Sovietskaya Ulitsa 28, tel: 329-8018, fax: 329-8019; e-mail: ryh@rh.ru; www.ryh.ru This American-run hostel offers cheap and clean rooms, and has a helpful travel bureau.

Camping

Retur Motel-Camping, Bolshaya Kupalnaya ulitsa 28, Town of Sestroretsk, tel: 437-7533; www.retur.ru One of the closest place to the city.

INTERNET CAFÉS

Most Internet cafés are open 24 hours, and are centrally located. Rates are reasonable, a little more than $2 per hour.

Quo Vadis, Nevsky Prospekt 24; www.quovadis.ru Hip café; great place to hang out, centrally located.

Café Max, Nevsky Prospekt 90; www.cafemax.ru Popular with student game players.

Red Fog, Kazanskaya Ulitsa 30; www.redfog.net Best rates; you can check your mail in 5 minutes for one ruble.

0

INDEX